A GUIDE T
PRAYE

A GUIDE TO
PRAYER

Isaac Watts

THE BANNER OF TRUTH TRUST

THE BANNER OF TRUTH TRUST
3 Murrayfield Road, Edinburgh EH12 6EL
P.O. Box 621, Carlisle, Pennsylvania 17013, USA

© The Banner of Truth Trust 2001
A Guide to Prayer first published 1715
First Banner of Truth Edition 2001

ISBN 0 85151 813 3

Typeset in 11/13pt Bembo at
The Banner of Truth Trust

Printed and bound in Great Britain by
Creative Print and Design (Wales),
Ebbw Vale

Contents

Preface

A Short Account of the Design
of this Treatise

Prayer is so great and necessary a part of religion that every degree of assistance in it will be always acceptable to pious minds. The inward and spiritual performance of this worship is taught us in many excellent discourses, but a regular scheme of prayer as a Christian exercise or a piece of holy skill, has been much neglected. The form, method and expression, together with other aspects of it, such as voice and gesture, have been so little treated that few Christians have any clear or distinct knowledge of them. Yet all these have all too powerful an influence upon the soul in its most spiritual exercises, and both nature and Scripture provide various directions about them. Now while institutes of logic and rhetoric abound that teach us to reason aright and to speak well among men, why should the rules of speaking to God be so little taught?

It is a glory to our profession that a great number of ministers in our day and nation are happy in the gift of prayer and exercise it continually in an honourable and useful manner. Yet they have been contented to direct others to it merely by the influence of a good example. Thus we are taught to pray, as some profess to teach

French and Latin, i.e., only by rote. But those who learn by rule as well as by imitation are much better prepared to speak those languages properly upon every occasion.

I am persuaded that one reason of this neglect has been the angry zeal for factions among us, which has discouraged men of sober and moderate principles from attempting much on this subject, while the zealots are divided into two extremes. Some contend earnestly for pre-composed, set forms of prayer and will worship God in no other way. These have little need of any other instructions but to be taught to read well, since the words, content and method of their prayers are already appointed. Other impassioned men, in extreme opposition to them, have indulged the irregular wanderings of thought and expression, lest by a confinement to rules they should seem to restrain the Spirit and return to carnal ordinances.

But if the leaders of one party had spent as much time in learning to pray as they have done in reading liturgies and vindicating their imposition; and if the vehement writers of the other side, together with the just cautions against quenching the Spirit, had more cultivated this divine skill themselves, and taught Christians regularly, how to pray; I believe the practice of free prayer would be more universally approved, and the fire of this controversy would never have raged to the destruction of so much charity.

My design in this treatise has been to write a prayer-book without forms. And I have sought to maintain the middle way between the distant mistakes of contending Christians.

In describing the nature of prayer, I have not enlarged much on each particular, nor made many subdivisions. Yet I have taken the greatest care and exactness to divide the duty into all its necessary parts, that the memory of younger Christians might be always furnished with some proper content and method for their addresses to God.

The 'gift', 'grace' and 'spirit' of prayer, have in recent years been made the subject of much ridicule. Some have utterly abandoned all pretences to them and turned the very terms to derision and reproach. But it must be confessed that others have given too just occasion for such scandal by explaining these words in a sense so exalted that they would be fitting only for divine inspiration. I have endeavoured therefore to reduce these terms to their more proper and rational meaning and explain them in such a way as the wisest and best men of all persuasions, who have not been stirred up with party zeal, have generally allowed. And I have had in view this design: that plainer Christians among the dissenters might understand what they themselves mean when they speak of praying by a gift and praying by the Spirit; and that they might not expose themselves to the criticism of talking without a meaning, or be accused of fanaticism by their conforming neighbours.

In speaking of the gift or ability to pray, I have been broad and particular, both in directions for attaining it and in describing the mistakes and indecencies which people may be in danger of committing. I am well assured that we learn to avoid what is culpable much better by a plain representation of faults and follies than by a bare proposal of the best rules and directions.

But here I am pressed between two difficulties and already feel the pain of displeasing some of my readers. If I should describe these improprieties of speech and action in a moderate degree, scoffers would criticise a whole party of Christians and say that my examples were taken from real life; while my friends would be ready to suspect that I had published some of the errors of weaker brethren. On the other hand, if I should present these faults at their most offensive, the adversary would scarcely believe that any preacher in our day was guilty of them; but my friends would tell me I was being irrelevant by exposing faults that nobody practises.

Now when two evils lie before me, I would rather choose the least. It is better to be irrelevant than to publicise folly. Therefore I have set forth those indecencies in their very worst appearance, that they might never be practised. To do this, I have borrowed instances of improper expressions from antiquated writers; and several of the descriptions of irregular voices and gesture are from obscure persons of the last age, whose talent of assurance was almost the only qualification that made them speakers in public. This I was constrained to do, because the prayers I have heard and observed could never have satisfied my design.

Moreover, had I described some tolerable follies, weak men might perhaps have been ready to vindicate them, not seeing deformity enough to be blamed. But now the instances I have given appear so disagreeable and ridiculous that all must be convinced that they ought to be avoided; and younger Christians when they learn to pray will keep at the greatest distance from all such examples. But it is a hard matter to attempt reformation of any kind without giving offence.

So that this work might not appear incomplete, I have also added one short chapter of the grace of prayer, though that subject has been abundantly pursued in many treatises and is the subject of daily sermons.

In speaking of the Spirit of prayer, I have tried to obviate all controversies that have arisen to trouble the church, by giving what appeared to me the most natural exposition of the chief scriptures that refer to this matter; and by adding a reasonable and intelligible account of the role of the Spirit of God in assisting his people in prayer.

At the end of these chapters I have laid down many rules, borrowed from reason, observations and holy Scripture, how every Christian may to some degree attain these desirable blessings. I have concluded the whole, with a sincere appeal to covet the best gifts and to seek after the most excellent way of performing this duty.

Perhaps some persons may wonder why, in a treatise that professes to teach the skill of prayer, I should not once recommend the prayer that our Lord taught his disciples as a perfect pattern for all Christians. But it is my opinion that divine wisdom gave it for other purposes. If this treatise meets with acceptance, I may then venture to publicise my thoughts on the Lord's prayer (if God shall ever give me health to review and finish them), together with a short essay or two on the personal ministry of Christ upon earth, which should properly be joined with them.

These institutes were first composed for the use of a private society of younger men who desired to learn to pray, and this may excuse the style in some parts of the work. It has lain silent by me several years and has resisted many a call to appear in public, in hopes of being more polished before its first appearance. But only God knows, whose hand has long confined me, when I shall have health and leisure to dress all my thoughts to the best advantage. I am at last convinced that it is better for me to do something for God, though it be imperfect, than to be guilty of perpetual delays in hopes of better pleasing myself.

I have taken the greatest care to avoid controversy and express myself in such a way as might not be justly offensive to any sober Christians. Yet if it should prove, unhappily, that I have said anything disagreeable to the sentiments of some of my younger readers, I must entreat them not to throw away the whole treatise and deprive themselves of all the benefit they might obtain by other parts of it. Nor should they load the whole book with criticisms, lest they prevent others from reaping those advantages toward converse with God which might be conveyed in the more inoffensive pages. An unwary censure, or a rash and hasty word thrown upon a discourse or a sermon, a writer or a preacher, has sometimes done more disservice to religion than could ever be compensated by many recantations. Permit this little book, whose honest design is to teach creatures to hold correspondence with their God, permit it to do all the service that it can.

Had I found any treatise that had satisfied my design, I would never have given myself the trouble of writing this in the first place or ventured to publish it now. There are indeed several well-composed forms of devotion in the world, written by ministers of the conformist and non-conformist persuasion. These are of excellent use to instruct us in the content and language of prayer, if we maintain our holy liberty and do not tie our thoughts down to the words of men. Mr Henry's *Method for Prayer*[1] is a judicious collection of scriptures pertaining to the several aspects of it. There is also a a volume of addresses to God which the author has entitled *Closet devotions on the principal heads of divinity, in the expressions of Scripture.* Both of these, if rightly used, will give valuable help to

[1] Matthew Henry's *A Method for Prayer* is again in print, from Christian Focus Publications.

the humble and serious worshipper. Those six sermons on prayer, published since this was written, are the useful labours of some of my valued friends, and they contain many divine thoughts. But they take in the whole range of this subject, in all the inward as well as the outward parts of the worship, and therefore could not allow sufficient room to enlarge upon my own chief design.

It is not necessary to inform the world that Bishop Wilkins, in his discourse of the gift of prayer, has been my chief assistant in the second chapter of this book. Nor need I tell my reader what writings I have consulted, in order to gain a clearer light, of the learned and pious Dr Owen and others who have written for or against the work of the Spirit in prayer. And I need not say what hints I have borrowed from the treatise of a very judicious author, with a fanciful title imposed upon it by an unknown hand, and called the *Generation of Seekers*, in which several practical cases about the aids of the Spirit are handled broadly and well – though I have had the opportunity of knowing and consulting it only since this was in the press.

But if there are any advances made here beyond the labours of great men in the last age, I hope the world will justify this attempt. And if younger Christians by perusing these papers shall find themselves improved in the holy skill of prayer, when they get nearest to the throne of grace, I entreat them to put in one petition for the author, who has languished under great weakness for some years past and is cut off from all public service. If ever he be restored again, he shall rejoice in further labours for their good; and he shall share in the pleasure of their improvements and assist them in the work of praise.

Introduction

P RAYER is a word which has broad meaning in Scripture. It includes not only a request for mercies, but it denotes the address of a creature on earth to God in heaven about everything that concerns his God, his neighbour or himself, in this world or the world to come. It is the conversation which God allows us to maintain with himself above, while we are here below. It is that language in which a creature communicates with his Creator and in which the soul of a saint often gets near to God, experiences great delight and, as it were, dwells with his heavenly Father for a short time before he comes to heaven. It is a glorious privilege with which our Maker has indulged us, as well as a necessary part of the obedience which he requires of us at all times and in every circumstance of life. 'Pray without ceasing' (*1 Thess. 5:17*). 'In everything by prayer and supplication, with thanksgiving, let your requests be made known unto God' (*Phil.* 4:6). 'Praying always with all prayer and supplication' (*Eph.* 6:18).

Prayer is a part of divine worship that is required of all men, and is to be performed either with the voice or only in the heart, and is called vocal or mental prayer. It is commanded to individuals in their private lives, in a more solemn and consistent manner; and in the midst of the businesses of life, by secretly and suddenly lifting up the soul to God. It belongs also to communities, whether they be natural, as families; or civil, as corporations, parliaments, courts, or societies for trade and business; and to religious communities. When persons meet together for any godly purpose, they should seek their God. It is required of the churches especially, for the house of God is the house of prayer.

Since it is a duty of such absolute necessity for all and of such universal use, it is fitting we should all know how to perform it aright, that it may be accepted by the great God, and become a delightful and profitable exercise to our own souls and to those that join with us.

I shall deliver my thoughts on the nature of prayer in the following order:

i. as a duty of worship;

ii. as it is to be performed by the gifts or abilities God has bestowed upon us;

iii. as it must be attended with the exercise of our graces; and

iv. as we are assisted in it by the Spirit of God.

I shall then conclude with an earnest address to Christians to seek after this holy skill of conversation with God.

Chapter I

The Nature of Prayer

I n speaking of prayer as a duty of worship required of us, we may, in order to understand the whole nature of prayer better, divide it into several parts. I think these may all be included in the following: invocation, adoration, confession, petition, pleading, profession (or self-dedication), thanksgiving and blessing. I shall speak of each particularly.

Invocation

THE FIRST PART of prayer is invocation, or calling upon God. It may include these three things:

1. *Mention of one or more of the names or titles of God.* In this way we indicate and acknowledge the person to whom we pray. There are abundant instances of this in the prayers that are recorded in holy Scripture, 'O Lord my God, most high and most holy God and Father'; 'O God of Israel, that dwellest between the cherubim'; 'Almighty God, the everlasting King'; 'Our Father which art in heaven'; 'O God, that keepest covenant'; and many others.

2. *A declaration of our desire and design to worship him.* 'Unto thee do we lift up our souls. We draw near unto thee as our God. We come into thy presence. We that are but

dust and ashes take upon us to speak to thy majesty. We bow ourselves before thee in humble addresses', or such like. And here it may not be amiss to mention briefly one or two general expressions of our own unworthiness.

3. *A desire of his assistance and acceptance,* under a sense of our own insufficiency and unworthiness, in such language as this:'Lord, quicken us to call upon thy name. Assist us by thy Spirit in our access to thy mercy-seat. Raise our hearts towards thyself.Teach us to approach thee as becomes creatures, and do thou draw near to us as a God of grace."Hearken to the voice of my cry, my king and my God, for unto thee will I pray"' (*Psa.* 5:2). In these words, all these three parts of invocation are expressed.

Adoration

THE SECOND PART of prayer is adoration, or honour paid to God by the creature. It contains these four things:

1. *A mention of his nature as God,* with the highest admiration and reverence.This includes his most original properties and perfections, namely, his self-sufficient existence, that he is God of and from himself; his unity of essence, that there is no other God besides himself; his inconceivable subsistence in three persons, the Father, the Son and the Holy Spirit, which mystery of the Trinity is a most proper object of our adoration and wonder, since it so much surpasses our understanding. His incomprehensible distance from all creatures and his infinite superiority of nature above them seem also to claim a place here.The language of this part of prayer runs thus:'Thou art God, and there is none else, thy name alone is Jehovah the most high. Who in the heavens can be compared to the Lord, or who among the sons of the mighty can be likened to our God? All nations before thee are as nothing,

and they are counted in thy sight less than nothing and vanity. Thou art the first and the last, the only true and living God; thy glorious name is exalted above all blessing and praise.'

2. *The mention of his many attributes,* with due expressions of praise and with the exercise of suitable grace and affection, as his power, his justice, his wisdom, his sovereignty, his holiness, his goodness and mercy. There is an abundance of this sort of expression in Scripture in those addresses that the saints have made to God in all ages: 'Thou art very great, O Lord, thou art clothed with honour and majesty. Thou art the blessed and only potentate, king of kings, and lord of lords. All things are naked and open before thine eyes. Thou searchest the heart of man, but how unsearchable is thine under-standing, and thy power is unknown. Thou art of purer eyes than to behold iniquity. Thy mercy endureth forever. Thou art slow to anger, abundant in goodness, and thy truth reaches to all generations.' These meditations are of great use in the beginning of our prayers, to abase us before the throne of God, to awaken our reverence, our dependence, our faith and hope, our humility and joy.

3. *The mention of his many works,* of creation, of providence and of grace, with proper praises. For as God is glorious in himself, his nature and his attributes, so by the works of his hands he has manifested that glory to us. And it becomes us to ascribe the same glory to him, that is, to tell him humbly that we are aware of the many perfections he has revealed in these works of his. We may use such language as this: 'Thou, Lord, hast made the heavens and the earth. The whole creation is the work of thine hands. Thou rulest among the armies of heaven, and among the inhabitants of the earth and thou doest what

pleases thee. Thou hast revealed thy goodness towards mankind, and hast magnified thy mercy above all thy name. Thy works of nature and of grace are full of wonder, and sought out by all those that have pleasure in them.'

4. *The mention of his relation to us* as a creator, as a father, as a redeemer, as a king, as an almighty friend, and our everlasting portion. And here it will not be improper to make mention of the name of Christ, in and through whom alone we are brought nigh to God and made his children; by whose incarnation and atonement he becomes a God and Father to sinful men and appears their reconciled friend. And by this means we draw still nearer to God in every part of this work of adoration.

When we consider his nature, we stand afar off from him as creatures from a God, for he is infinitely superior to us. When we speak of his attributes a great acquaintance seems to grow between God and us, while we tell him that we have learned something of his power, his wisdom, his justice and his mercy. But when we proceed to mention the many works of his hands, by which he has tangibly revealed himself to our understanding, we seem to approach yet nearer to God. And when at last we can arise to call him our God, from a sense of his special relation to us in Christ, then we gain the nearest access and are better prepared for the following parts of this worship.

Confession

THE THIRD PART of prayer consists in confession. This may be divided into these four heads:

1. *A humble confession of the lowliness of our original nature;* our distance from God, as we are creatures; our subjection to him; and our constant dependence on him.

'Thou, O Lord, art in heaven, but we on the earth; our being is but of yesterday, and our foundation is in the dust. What is man that thou art mindful of him, and the son of man that thou shouldest visit him? Man, that is a worm, and the son of man, that is but a worm! It is in thee that we live, move and have our being: thou withholdest thy breath and we die.'

2. *A confession of our sins:* both original, which belong to our nature; and actual, that have been found in the course of our lives. We should confess our sins under the sense of the guilt of them, as well as under the deep and mournful impressions of the power of sin in our hearts. We should confess the sins that we have been guilty of in thought, as well as the iniquities of our lips and of our lives; our sins of omission and sins of commission; the sins of our childhood and of our riper years; sins against the law of God and sins more particularly committed against the gospel of our Lord Jesus Christ.

Sometimes it is convenient and necessary to enter into a more particular detail of our various faults and follies. We should mourn before God because of our pride and vanity of mind; the intensity of our passions; our earthly-mindedness and love of this world; our indulgence of our flesh; our carnal security and unthankfulness under plentiful mercies, and our fretfulness and impatience, or sinful dejection, in a time of trouble; our neglect of duty and lack of love to God; our unbelief and hardness of heart; our slothfulness and decay in religion; the dishonours we have brought to God; and all our failures towards our fellow creatures. And these may be aggravated on purpose to humble our souls yet more before God, by reflecting on their variety and their number: how often they have been repeated even before and since we knew God savingly; that we have committed them against much light and have sinned against much love; and we have committed these after many rebukes of the Word and providence and many consolations from the gospel and the Spirit of God. This part of prayer is very frequently insisted and enlarged upon among those examples that are left us in the Word of God.

And with these confessions, we must lament and take shame to ourselves. 'We are ashamed, and blush to lift up our faces before thee our God, for our iniquities are increased over our head and our trespasses grown up to the heavens. See, we are contemptible; what shall we answer thee? We will lay our hands upon our mouth and put our mouth in the dust, if so be there may be hope.'

3. *A confession, arising from our sense of all our aggravated sins, that we deserve punishment* and are unworthy of mercy. We may use such expressions as these: 'We deserve, O Lord, to be forever cast out of thy presence, and to be eternally cut off from all hope of mercy. We deserve to fall under the curse of that law which we have broken and to be forever banished from the blessings of that gospel which we have so long refused. We have sinned against so much mercy that we are no longer worthy to be called thy children. We are utterly unworthy of any of those favours that are promised in thy Word and which thou hast given us encouragement to hope for. If thou contend with us for our transgressions, we are not able to answer thee, O Lord, nor to make excuse for one of a thousand. If thou shouldest mark iniquities, O Lord, who shall stand? But there is forgiveness with thee, there is mercy and plenteous redemption.'

4. *A confession or humble representation of our wants and sorrow of every kind.* The particulars of this will fall under

the next section, but it is necessary that they should be spread before God and poured out in his presence, for God loves to hear us tell him how we feel about our own particular necessities and troubles. He loves to hear us complain before him when we are under any pressures from his hand or when we stand in need of mercies of any kind.

Petition

THE FOURTH PART of prayer consists of petition, which includes in it a desire of deliverance from evil (called deprecation), and a request of good things to be bestowed (sometimes called comprecation). For both of these we must offer up our petitions to God for ourselves and our fellow creatures.

The evils we pray to be delivered from are of a temporal, spiritual or eternal kind. 'O Lord, take away the guilt of our sins by the atonement of thine own Son. Subdue the power of our iniquities by thy own Spirit. Deliver us from the natural darkness of our own minds, from the corruption of our hearts, and from perverse tendencies of our appetites and passions. Free us from the temptations to which we are exposed and the daily snares that attend us. We are in constant danger whilst we are in this life, let the watchful eye of our God be upon us for our defence. Deliver us from thine everlasting wrath and from that eternal punishment in hell that is due to our sins. Save us from the power of our enemies in this world and from all the painful evils that we have justly exposed ourselves to by sinning against thee.'

The good we desire to be conferred upon us is also of a temporal, spiritual or eternal nature. As we pray for the pardon of all our iniquities for the sake of the great atonement, the death of our Redeemer, so we beg of God our justification through the righteousness of his own Son Jesus Christ and our acceptance with God unto eternal life. We pray for the sanctification of our natures by his Holy Spirit, for his enlightening influences to teach us the knowledge of God in Christ Jesus, as well as to reveal to us the evil of sin and our danger by it. We pray for the consolation of the Spirit of God, and that he would not only work faith and love and every grace in our hearts, but give us bright and plentiful evidences of his own work and of our own interest in the love of God.

We say unto God, 'O thou that hast the hearts of all men in thine hand, form our hearts according to thine own will and according to the image of thine own Son. Be our light and our strength; make us run in the ways of holiness. Let all the means of grace be continued to us and be made serviceable for the great end for which thou hast appointed them. Preserve thy gospel among us, and let all thy providences be sanctified. Let thy mercies draw us nearer to thyself as with the cords of love, and let the strokes of thine afflicting hand wean us from sin, mortify us to this world, and make us ready for a departure, whenever thou pleasest to call us. Guide us by thy counsels; secure us by thy grace in all our travels through this dangerous wilderness; and at last give us a triumph over death and a rich and abundant entrance into the kingdom of thy Son in glory.

'But since while we are here we wear these bodies of flesh, and there are many things necessary to support our lives and to make them comfortable, we entreat thee that thou wouldst bestow these conveniences and refreshments upon us, so far as is consistent with thine own glory and the designs of thy grace. Let our health, our strength and our peace be maintained, and let holiness to the Lord be inscribed upon them all, that whatever we receive from thine hands may be used to thine honour and our own truest advantage. Heal our diseases and pardon our iniquities, that our souls may ever bless thee.'

And as we are required to offer up petitions for ourselves and make our own requests known to God, so we are commanded to make supplication for all saints (*Eph.* 6:18) and to offer up prayers and intercessions for all men (*1 Tim.* 2:1). 'Intercession' is the common name for this part of our petitions.

In general, we must pray for the church of Christ, for Zion lies near to the heart of God and her name is written upon the palms of the hands of our Redeemer. The welfare of Zion should be much upon our hearts; we ought always to have the tenderest concern for the whole church of God in the world. His church he values above kingdoms and nations. Therefore, if we distinguish degrees of fervency in prayer, we ought to plead with God for his church more earnestly than for any nation or kingdom, that he would enlarge the borders of the dominion of Christ; that he would spread his gospel among the heathen and make the name of Christ known and glorious from the rising of the sun to its going down; that he would call in the remainder of his ancient people, the Jews; that he would bring the fullness of the Gentiles into his church; and that he would pour down a more abundant measure of his own Spirit to carry on his own work upon the earth. And we are to send up longing and earnest wishes to heaven that the Spirit may descend and be diffused in plentiful degrees upon churches, upon ministers, upon families, and upon all the saints. We are to pray that God would deliver his church from the power of persecuting enemies, and that he would restrain the wrath of man and not allow the wicked to triumph over the righteous.

We are also in particular to request of God mercy for the nation to which we belong, that liberty and peace may be established and flourish in it; for governors that rule over us in places of supreme or subordinate authority; and that wisdom and faithfulness may be conferred upon them from heaven to manage those affairs God has entrusted them with on earth. We must pray for our friends and near relations, that God would deliver them from all the evils they feel or fear and bestow upon them all the good we wish for ourselves here or hereafter.

There is also another kind of petition which is used frequently in the Old Testament, and that is imprecation, or a calling for vengeance and destruction upon enemies. But this is very seldom to be used under the gospel, which is a dispensation of love. It should never be employed against our personal enemies, but only against the enemies of Christ and such as are irreconcilable to him. Christ taught us in his life, and gave us an example at his death, to forgive and pray for our personal enemies, for that is a noble singularity and glory of our religion.

Here let it be observed that when we pray for those things which are absolutely necessary to the glory of God or to our own salvation, we may use a fuller and more fervent importunity in prayer. We may say, 'Lord, without the pardon of our sins we cannot rest satisfied; without the renovation of our natures by thy grace, our souls can never rest easy; without the hopes of heaven we can never be at peace; and in these respects will never let thee go till thou bless us. For Zion's sake we will not hold our peace, and for the sake of thy Jerusalem, thy glory, thy church in the world, we will give thee no rest till thou hast made her the joy of the earth.'

But on the other hand, when we plead with God for those mercies or comforts upon which our salvation or his own glory do not necessarily depend, we dare not use so absolute an importunity in prayer, but we must learn to limit our petitions in such language as this: 'If it be consistent with thine eternal counsels, with the purposes of grace, and the great ends of thy glory, then bestow upon us such a blessing. If it may be for the true interest of our souls and for thine honour in the world, then let this favour be granted to us. Otherwise we would learn to resign ourselves to thy wiser determination, and say, Father, not our wills, but thine be done.'

Pleading

THE FIFTH PART of prayer may be called pleading with God. Though this is not so distinct a part by itself, but rather belongs to the work of petition and request, it is so very large and diffusive that it may well be treated separately.

Pleading with God, or arguing our case with him in a fervent yet humble manner, is one part of that importunity in prayer which Scripture so much recommends. This is what all the saints of old have practised. This is what Job resolves to engage in: If I could get nearer to God, 'I would order my cause before him, and fill my mouth with arguments' (*Job* 23:3–4). This is what the prophet Jeremiah practises: 'Righteous art thou, O Lord, when I plead with thee: yet let me talk with thee of thy judgments: Wherefore doth the way of the wicked prosper?' (*Jer.* 12:1). We are not to suppose that our arguments can have any real influence on God's own will and persuade him contrary to what he was before inclined.

But as he condescends to talk with us after the manner of men, so he admits us to talk with him in the same manner and encourages us to plead with him as though he were inwardly and really moved and prevailed upon by our importunities. So Moses is said to have prevailed upon God for the preservation of his people Israel, when he seemed resolved upon their destruction (*Exod.* 32:7–14). In this work of pleading with God, arguments are almost infinite, but the chief of them may be reduced to these following headings:

1. *We may plead with God from the greatness of our wants, our dangers or our sorrows,* whether they relate to the soul or the body, to this life or the life to come, to ourselves or those for whom we pray. We may draw arguments for deliverance from the particular kind of afflictions that we labour under. 'My sorrows, O Lord, overpress me and endanger my dishonouring of thy name and thy gospel. My pains and my weaknesses hinder me from thy service, that I am rendered useless upon earth and a burden to the earth. They have already continued so long that I fear my flesh will not be able to hold out, nor my spirit to bear up, if thine hand abide thus heavy upon me. If this sin is not subdued in me, or that temptation removed, I fear I shall be turned aside from the paths of religion and let go my hope.' Thus from the kind, degree or duration of our difficulties, we may draw arguments for relief.

2. *The many perfections of the nature of God* provide another kind of argument in prayer: 'For thy mercies' sake, O Lord, save me. Thy lovingkindness is infinite; let this infinite lovingkindness be displayed in my salvation. Thou art wise, O Lord; though mine enemies are crafty, thou canst disappoint their devices, and thou knowest how by thy wondrous counsels to turn my sorrows into joy. Thou

canst find out a way for my relief when all creatures stand afar off and say that they see no way to help me. Thou art almighty and all-sufficient; thy power can suppress my adversaries at once, vanquish the tempter, break the powers of darkness to pieces, release me from the chains of my corruption, and bring me into glorious liberty. Thou art just and righteous; wilt thou let the enemy oppress forever? Thou art sovereign, and all things are at thy command. Thou canst say to pains and diseases, Go, or Come; speak therefore the sovereign word of healing, and my flesh and soul shall praise thee. Thou delightest in pardoning grace; it is the honour of our God to forgive. Therefore let my iniquities all be cancelled through the abundance of thy rich mercy.'

3. *Another argument in pleading with God may be drawn from the several relations in which God stands to men,* particularly to his own people. 'Lord, thou art my Creator; wilt thou not have a desire to the work of thine hands? Hast thou not made me and fashioned me, and wilt thou now destroy me? Thou art my governor and my king; to whom should I fly for protection but to thee, when the enemies of thine honour and my soul beset me around? Art thou not my father, and hast thou not called me one of thy children and given me a name and a place among thy sons and daughters? Why should I look like one cast out of thy sight, or one who belongs to the family of Satan? Hast thou not the heart of a father and tender compassions? Why should one of thy poor and weak helpless children be neglected or forgotten? Art thou not my God in covenant, and the God and Father of my Lord Jesus Christ, by whom that covenant is ratified? Under that relation, I would plead with thee for all necessary mercies.'

4. *The various and particular promises of the covenant of grace* form another class of arguments to use in prayer. 'Enlighten me, O Lord, and pardon me, and sanctify my soul. Bestow grace and glory upon me according to that word of thy promise on which thou hast caused me to hope. Remember thy word is past in heaven; it is recorded among the articles of thy sweet covenant, that I must receive light and love, and strength and joy and happiness. Art thou not a faithful God to fulfil every one of those promises? What if heaven and earth must pass away? Yet thy covenant stands upon two immutable pillars, thy promise and thine oath. Now I have fled for refuge to lay hold on this hope; let me have strong consolation. Remember the covenant made with thy Son in the days of eternity, and let the mercies there promised to all his seed be bestowed upon me according to my various wants.' This recalling of the covenant of God has often been greatly prevalent and efficacious in the prayers of the ancient saints.

5. *The name and honour of God in the world* is another powerful argument. 'The Canaanites shall cut off our name from the earth; and what wilt thou do unto thy great name?' (*Josh.* 7:9). If thy saints go down to the grave in multitudes, who shall praise thee in the land of the living? 'Death can not celebrate thee. The living, he shall praise thee, as I do this day.' This was the pleading of Hezekiah (*Isa.* 38:18–19). And David uses the same language in Psalm 6:5. 'For thy name's sake' was a mighty argument in all the ancient times of the church.

6. *Former experiences of ourselves and others* are another set of arguments to make use of in prayer. Our Lord Jesus Christ in that prophetic psalm is represented as using this argument: '"Our fathers trusted in thee, and

thou didst deliver them. They cried unto thee, and were not confounded" (*Psa.* 22:4–5). Let me be a partaker of the same favour whilst I cry unto thee and make thee my trust. Thou hast never said to the seed of Jacob, Seek ye my face in vain; and let it not be said that thy poor servant has now sought thy face and hast not found thee. Often have I received mercy in response to prayer. Often hath my soul drawn near unto thee and been comforted in the midst of sorrows. Often have I taken out fresh supplies of grace according to my need from the treasures of thy grace that are in Christ. Shall the door of these treasures be shut against me now? Shall I receive no more favours from the hand of my God, who has before dealt them so plentifully to me?'

Now, however improper this sort of argument may seem in courts of princes, or to entreat the favour of great men, God loves to hear his own people make use of it. For though men are quickly weary of multiplying their bounties, the more we receive from God, if we humbly acknowledge it to him, the more we are likely to receive still.

7. *The most powerful and most prevailing argument is the name and mediation of our Lord Jesus Christ.* And though there are some hints or shadows of it in the Old Testament, it was never taught us in a plain and express manner till a little before our Saviour left this world: 'Hitherto have ye asked nothing in my name: ask, and ye shall receive, that your joy may be full. Whatsoever ye shall ask the Father in my name, he will give it you' (*John* 16:24, 23). This seems to be reserved for the peculiar pleasure and power of the duty of prayer under the gospel. We are taught to make mention of the name of Jesus, the only begotten and eternal Son of God, as a

method to receive our biggest requests and fullest salvation.

In such language as this we should address the Father: 'Lord, let my sins be forgiven, for the sake of that love which thou bearest thine own Son; for the sake of that love which thy Son beareth to thee; for the sake of his humble state when he took flesh upon him, that he might look like a sinner and be made a sacrifice, though himself was free from sin; for the sake of his perfect and painful obedience, which has given complete honour to thy law; for the sake of the curse which he bore and the death which he suffered, which hath glorified thine authority and honoured thy justice more than it was possible for my sins to have affronted it. Remember his dying groans; remember his agonies when the hour of darkness was upon him; and do not let the powers of darkness prevail over me. Remember the day when thou stoodest afar from thine own Son and he cried out as one forsaken of God; and let me have thine everlasting presence with me. Let me never be forsaken, since thy Son hath borne that punishment.'

Again, we may plead with God the intercession of Jesus, our High Priest above: 'Father, we would willingly ask thee for nothing, but what thy Son already asks thee for. We would willingly request nothing at thine hands, but what thine own Son requests beforehand for us. Look upon the Lamb, as he had been slain, in the midst of the throne; look upon his pure and perfect righteousness and that blood with which our High Priest is entered into the highest heavens, and in which forever he appears before thee to make intercession. Let every blessing be bestowed upon me which that blood did purchase and which that great, that infinite, petitioner pleads for at thy right hand. What canst thou deny thine own Son? For he hath told us, that thou hearest him always. For the sake of that Son of thy love, deny us not.'

Profession, or Self-Dedication

THE SIXTH PART of prayer consists in a profession or self-dedication.

This is very seldom mentioned by writers as a part of prayer, but to me it appears so very necessary and so distinct from all the rest that it ought to be treated separately as well as any other part. It may be divided under these four heads:

1. *A profession of our relationship to God.* It is worth-while sometimes for a saint to draw near to God and to tell him that he is the Lord's; that he belongs to his family; that he is one of his household; that he stands among the number of his children; that his name is written in his covenant. A great deal of spiritual delight and soul-satisfaction arises from such appeals to God concerning our relation to him.

2. *A profession of our former transactions with God.* 'Lord, we have given ourselves up unto thee and chosen thee for our eternal portion and our highest good. We have seen the insufficiency of creatures to make us happy, and we have betaken ourselves to a higher hope. We have beheld Christ Jesus the Saviour in his perfect righteousness and in his all-sufficient grace. We have put our trust in him, and we have made our covenant with the Father, by the sacrifice of his Son. We have often drawn near to thee in thine ordinances. We have ratified and confirmed the holy covenant at thy table, as well as been devoted to thee by the initial ordinance of baptism. We have given up our names to God in his house, and we have as it were subscribed with our hands to be the Lord's.'

3. *A present surrender of ourselves to God and a profession of the present exercise of our affections and graces towards him.* This is sweet language in prayer, when the soul is in a right frame. 'Lord, I confirm all my former dedications of myself to thee; and may all my covenantings be forever ratified. Or if I did never yet sincerely give myself up to the Lord, I do it now with the greatest solemnity, and from the bottom of my heart. I commit my guilty soul into the hands of Jesus my Redeemer, that he may sprinkle it with his atoning blood, that he may clothe it with his justifying righteousness and make me, a vile sinner, accepted in the presence of a just and holy God. I appear, O Father, in the presence of thy justice and holiness, clothed in the garments of thine own Son, and I trust thou beholdest not iniquity in me to punish it. I give my soul, that has much corruption in it by nature, and much of the remaining power of sin, into the hands of my almighty Saviour, that by his grace he may form all my powers anew; that he may subdue every irregular appetite and root out every disorderly passion; that he may frame me after his own image, fill me with his own grace, and fit me for his own glory. I hope in thee, my God, for thou art my refuge, my strength, and my salvation. I love thee above all things, and I know I love thee. Whom have I in heaven but thee? and there is none upon earth that I desire in comparison of thee. I desire thee with my strongest affections, and I delight in thee above all delights. My soul stands in awe and fears before thee; and I rejoice to love such a God who is almighty and the object of my highest reverence.'

4. *A profession of our humble and holy resolutions to be the Lord's forever.* This is what is generally called a vow. Now, I cannot encourage Christians to bind themselves in

particular instances by frequently repeated vows, and especially in things that are in themselves indifferent; this often proves a dangerous snare to souls. Yet we can never be too frequent or too solemn in the general surrender of our souls to God and binding our souls by a vow to be the Lord's forever: to love him above all things, to fear him, to hope in him, to walk in his ways in a course of holy obedience, and to wait for his mercy unto eternal life. For such a vow as this is included in the nature of both the ordinances of the gospel, baptism and the Lord's Supper. Such a vow as this is comprehended in almost every act of worship, and especially in solemn addresses to God by prayer.

I might add, lastly, that together with this profession or self-dedication to God, it is necessary that we should renounce everything that is inconsistent with this or with anything under the four preceding heads: 'I am thine, O Lord, and I do not belong to this world. I have given myself to thee, and I have given myself away from sin and from the creature. I have renounced the world as my portion and chosen the Father. I have renounced all other saviours and all my own duties and righteousness as the foundation of my interest in the favour of God, and chosen Christ Jesus as my only way to the Father. I have renounced my own strength as the ground of my hope; for my understanding is dark, my will is impotent, and my best affections are insufficient to carry me onwards to heaven. I now again renounce dependence upon all of them, that I may receive greater light and strength and love from God. I am dead to the law, I am mortified to sin, I am crucified to the world, and all by the cross of Jesus my Saviour. I bid Satan get behind me; I renounce him and his works. I will neither fear him nor love him, nor lay a confederacy with the men of this world, for I love my God, for I fear my God, and in my God is my eternal help and hope. I will say, What have I to do any more with idols?, and I will banish the objects of temptation from my sight. Thus I abandon everything that would divide me from God, to whom I have made a surrender of myself. And shouldest thou see fit to scourge and correct me, O my God, I submit to thine hand. Shouldest thou deny me the particular requests I have presented to thee, I leave myself in thy hands, trusting thou wilt choose better for me. And because I know my own frailty of heart and the inconstancy of my will, I humbly put all these my vows and solemn engagements into the hands of my Lord Jesus to fulfil them in me, and by me, through all the days of my infirmity and this dangerous state of trial.'

Thanksgiving

THE SEVENTH PART of prayer consists in thanksgiving. To give thanks is to acknowledge the bounty of that hand from which we receive our blessings, and to ascribe honour and praise to the power, the wisdom and the goodness of God upon that account. And this is part of that tribute which God our king expects at our hands for all the favours we receive from him. It very ill becomes a creature to partake of benefits from his God, and then to forget his heavenly benefactor and grow regardless of that bounty from which his comforts flow. Our thanksgivings may be arranged under two heads: we must give thanks for those benefits for which we have prayed, and for those which God has conferred upon us without praying for.

1. *Those benefits which God has bestowed on us without our asking* are proper to be mentioned in the first place,

for they are the effects of his rich and preventing mercy. How many are the blessings of his goodness with which he has prevented us! 'We praise thee, O Lord, for thine original designs of love to fallen man, that thou shouldest make a distinction between us and the angels that sinned. What is man, that thou art thoughtful about his salvation and sufferest the angels to perish forever without remedy; that thou shouldest choose a certain number of the race of Adam, and give them into the hands of Christ before all worlds and make a covenant of grace with them in Christ Jesus, that their happiness might be secured; that thou shouldest reveal this mercy in various types and promises to our fathers by the prophets and that in thine own appointed time thou shouldest send thy Son to take our nature upon him, and to redeem us by his death?

We give glory to thy justice and to thy grace for this work of terror and compassion, this work of reconciling sinners to thyself by the punishment of thy Son. We praise thee for the gospel which thou hast published to the world, the gospel of pardon and peace, and that thou hast confirmed it by such abundant testimonies to raise and establish our faith. We give glory to that power of thine that has guarded the gospel in all ages, and through ten thousand oppositions of Satan has delivered it down safe to our age, and has proclaimed the glad tidings of peace in our nation.

'We bless thee that thou hast built habitations for thyself amongst us, and that we should be born in such a land of light as this is. It is a distinguishing favour of thine that among the works of thy creation we should be placed in the rank of rational beings; but it is more distinguishing goodness that we should be born of religious parents under the general promises of grace. We give thanks unto thy goodness for our preservation from many dangers which we could never foresee and which we could not ask thee to prevent. How infinitely are we indebted to thee, O Lord, that thou hast not cut us off in a state of nature and sin, and that our portion is not at this time amongst the children of eternal wrath; that our education should be under religious care; that we should have so many conveniences and comforts of life conferred upon us, as well as the means of grace brought near to us; and all this before we began to know thee or sought any of the mercies of this life or the other at thine hands!'

2. *We must give thanks for the benefits we have received as an answer to prayer.* Whatever blessings we have sought at the hands of God demand our acknowledgments to his goodness when we become receivers. Here there is no need to enlarge in particulars, for we may look back upon the fourth part of prayer, which consists in petition, and there read the matter of our thankfulness. There we learn to give glory to God for our deliverance from evils temporal and spiritual and our hopes of deliverance from the evils that are eternal; for the communication of good for soul and body and our comfortable expectation of the eternal happiness of both; for mercies bestowed on churches, on nations, on our governors, on our relatives and friends, as well as ourselves. And we should rejoice in our praises and say to the Lord, 'Truly thou art a God that hearest prayer, and thou hast not despised the cry of those that sought thee. We ourselves are witnesses that thou dost not bid thy people seek thy face in vain.'

All our thanksgivings may be yet further heightened in prayer by considering the multitude of mercies that we have received, their greatness and their continuance; by mentioning the glory and self-sufficiency of God the giver: that he is happy in himself and stands in no need of us, and yet he condescends to confer perpetual benefits upon us; that he is sovereign and might dispose of his favours to thousands and leave us out of the number of his favourites. We are as vile and unworthy as others, and our God beholds all our unworthiness, all our guilt, our repeated provocations, and his past mercies abused, and yet he continues to have mercy upon us and waits to be gracious.

Blessing

THE EIGHTH PART of prayer consists in blessing of God, which has a sense distinct from praise or adoration and is distinguished also from thanksgiving. In Psalm 145:10 it is said, 'All thy works shall praise thee, O Lord; and thy saints shall bless thee.' That is, even the inanimate creation, which are the works of God, manifest his attributes and his praises, but his saints do something more: they bless his name. This part of worship consists in these two things:

1. *Mentioning the many attributes and glories of God with inward joy, satisfaction and pleasure.* 'We delight, O Lord, to see thy name honoured in the world, and we rejoice in thy real excellencies. We take pleasure to see thee exalted above all. We triumph in the many perfections of thy nature, and we give thanks at the remembrance of thine holiness.' Thus we rejoice and bless the Lord for what he is in himself, as well as for what he has done for us. This is a most divine and unselfish act of worship.

2. *Wishing the glories of God may forever continue, and rejoicing at the assurance of it.* 'May the name of God be forever blest; may the kingdom, and the power, and the glory be forever ascribed to him; may all generations call

him honourable and make his name glorious in the earth. To thee, O Father, Son, and Holy Spirit, belong everlasting power and honour.'

Amen, or the Conclusion

WE ARE TAUGHT in many places of Scripture to conclude our prayers with *Amen,* which is a Hebrew word that signifies truth or faithfulness, certainly, surely, etc. It implies these four things:

1. *A belief* of all that we have said concerning God and ourselves, of all our ascriptions of honour to God in the mention of his name, attributes and works; and an inward persuasion of our own unworthiness, our wants and our sorrows which we have before expressed.

2. *A wishing and desiring to obtain* all that we have prayed for, longing after it and looking for it. 'Lord, let it be thus as we have said' is the language of this little word Amen at the end of our prayers.

3. *A confirmation* of all our professions, promises and engagements to God. It is used as the form of the oath of God in some places in Scripture: 'Truly' or 'Surely blessing I will bless thee' (*Heb.* 6:13, 14). And it is, as it were, a solemn oath in our lips, binding ourselves to the Lord according to the professions that we have made in the foregoing part of worship.

4. *The hope and sure expectation* of the acceptance of our persons, and audience of our prayers. For while we thus confirm our dedication of ourselves to God, we also humbly lay claim to his accomplishment of the promises of his covenant, and expect and wait that he will fulfil all our petitions so far as they are agreeable to our truest interest and the designs of his own glory.

CHAPTER 2

The Gift of Prayer

Having spoken of the nature of prayer and divided it into its several parts, we proceed to address the gift or ability to pray.

This holy skill of speaking to God in prayer has usually been called a gift, and because of this it has been, by the weakness and folly of some persons, represented as being like the gift of miracles or prophecy, which are entirely the effects of divine inspiration, wholly out of our reach and unattainable by our utmost endeavours. Following this, the malice of others has taken occasion to reproach all claims of it as vain fancies and wild enthusiasm.

But I shall attempt to give so rational an account of it in the following sections and lay down such plain directions how to attain it with the assistance of the Holy Spirit and his blessing on our own diligence and labour, that I hope those prejudices will be removed and the unjust reproach be wiped away forever.

What the Gift of Prayer Is

THE GIFT OF PRAYER may be described as an ability to suit our thoughts to all the various parts and designs of this duty, and a readiness to express those thoughts before God in the fittest manner to profit our own souls as well as the souls of others that join with us.

It is called a gift, partly because it was bestowed on the apostles and primitive Christians in an immediate and extraordinary manner by the Spirit of God, and partly because the ordinary assistance of the Spirit of God is required even to attain this holy skill or ability to pray.

In the first propagation of the gospel, it pleased the Spirit of God to bestow various powers and abilities on believers, and these were called the gifts of the Spirit (*1 Cor.* 12:4, 8, 9). Such were the gifts of preaching, of exhortation, of psalmody, that is, the making and singing of psalms, of healing the sick, of speaking many tongues, etc. Now, though these were given to men at once in an extraordinary way then, and the habits wrought in them by immediate divine power made them capable of exerting the acts on just occasions, these powers or abilities of speaking many tongues, of psalmody, of preaching and healing, are now to be obtained by human diligence, with due dependence on the concurring blessing of God. And the same must be said concerning the gift or faculty of prayer.

As the art of medicine or healing is founded on the knowledge of natural principles and is made up of rules drawn from the nature of things and from reason and observation, so the art of preaching is learned and attained by the knowledge of divine principles and the use of rules and directions for explaining and applying divine truths; and so, too, the holy skill of prayer is built on a just knowledge of God and ourselves, and may be taught in as rational a method by proper directions and rules. But because in a special manner we expect the aid of the Holy Spirit in things so serious and sacred, the faculties of preaching and praying are called the gifts of the Spirit even to this day; whereas the word is not nowadays applied to the art of medicine or skill in the languages.

Forms of Prayer, Free or Conceived Prayer, and Praying Extempore

THE GIFT OF PRAYER is one of the noblest and most useful in the Christian life, and it is therefore to be sought with earnest desire and diligence. In order to attain it, we must avoid these two extremes: 1. Confining ourselves entirely to pre-composed forms of prayer; and 2. Entire dependence on sudden motions and suggestions of thought.

1. The first extreme to be avoided is confining ourselves to set, pre-composed forms of prayer.

I grant it is lawful and convenient for weaker Christians to use a form in prayer rather than not to perform that duty at all. Christ himself seems to have indulged it to his disciples in their infant state of Christianity (*Luke* 11:1–13). I grant also that sometimes the most improved saints may find their own wants and desires and the frames of their own hearts so well expressed in the words of other men that they cannot find better. They may therefore in a very pious manner use the same, especially when they labour under a present deadness of spirit and great indisposition for the duty. It is also evident that much assistance may be borrowed by younger and elder Christians from forms of prayer that are well composed, without using the whole form as a prayer. And if I may use the words of a judicious author who wrote more than forty years ago, I would say with him that 'forms may be useful, and in some cases necessary'. We say this because:

i. 'Some, even among Christians and professors, are so unlearned and ignorant, though it may be spoken to their shame, that they cannot tolerably express their desires in prayer; must such utterly neglect the duty? Is it not better in their gross ignorance to use the help of others' gifts and composures than not to pray at all, or to utter that which is senseless and impious? I speak it not to excuse their ignorance, nor to encourage them to rest satisfied in that condition, but for the present necessity.

ii. 'Some again can do it privately and so far as may suffice in their secret addresses to God; but when they are to pray before others, they lack either dexterity and fitness of expression, readiness of utterance, or confidence to use those abilities they have. Yet these I will not excuse from sinful bashfulness.

iii. 'It is possible that some bodily disorder or sudden distraction may befall such as are otherwise able and may becloud their minds, weaken their memories, and dull their parts, that they may be unfit to express themselves extemporaneously. This may happen in case of melancholy, cold palsies, or similar disorders.

'I conclude then, that in the cases aforesaid, or the like, a form may be profitable and helpful. Nor is it tying up the Spirit, but if conscionably used, may both be attended with the Spirit's assistance and find acceptance with God. Yet it will not follow that any should satisfy themselves in such stated and stinted forms, and much less that those who have praying abilities should be enforced by others to rest in them. If ignorance, bashfulness, defect of memory, or other disorder may render it excusable and necessary to some, is it fit that all should rest in their measure? Where then will be that earnest coveting of the best gifts? Or why should those that are excellently gifted that way be hindered from the use and exercise of that gift because others lack it?'

Thus far this worthy writer.

Now though the use of forms in such cases is not unlawful, a perpetual confinement to them will be accompanied by such difficulties as these:

1. *It much hinders the free exercise of our own thoughts and desires,* which is the chief work and business of prayer, namely, to express our desires to God. Whereas our thoughts and affections should direct our words, a set form of words directs our thoughts and affections. While we bind ourselves to those words only, we dampen our inward devotion and prevent the holy fire from kindling within us. We discourage our active powers and passions from running out on divine subjects, and we obstruct the breathings of our souls heavenward. The wise man tells us, 'The heart knoweth his own bitterness; and a stranger doth not intermeddle with his joy' (*Prov.* 14:10). There are secret joys and unknown bitterness which the holy soul longs to spread before God and for which it cannot find any exact and corresponding expressions in the best of prayer-books. Must such a Christian suppress all those thoughts, and forbid himself all that sweet conversation with his God, because it is not written down in the appointed form?

2. *The thoughts and affections of the heart that are truly pious and sincere are wrought in us by the Spirit of God.* If we deny them utterance because they are not found in prayer-books, we run the danger of resisting the Holy Ghost, quenching the Holy Spirit, and fighting against the kind designs of God towards us – these things which we are so expressly cautioned against (*1 Thess.* 5:19) and which a humble Christian trembles to think of.

3. *A confinement to forms cramps and imprisons those powers that God has given us for improvement and use.* It silences

our natural abilities and forbids them to act; it bars our spiritual faculties and prevents their growth. To satisfy ourselves with mere forms, to confine ourselves wholly to them and neglect to stir up and make use of our own gifts, is one kind of spiritual sloth and highly to be disapproved. It is hiding a talent in the earth which God has given us for the purpose of carrying on a trade with heaven. It is an abuse of our knowledge of divine things, to neglect the use of it in our converse with God. It is as if a man that had once used crutches to support him when he was feeble would always use them; or because he has sometimes found his own thoughts happily expressed in conversation by another person, will therefore assent to what that other person shall always say, and never speak his own thoughts himself.

4. *It leads us into the danger of hypocrisy and mere lip-service.* Sometimes we shall be tempted to express those things which are not the very thoughts of our own souls, and so use words that are not suited to our present wants, sorrows or requests, because those words are put together and made ready beforehand.

5. *The confinement of ourselves to a form, though not always attended with formality and indifference, is very apt to make our spirits cold and flat, formal and indifferent in our devotion.* The frequent repetition of the same words does not always awaken the same affections in our hearts, which perhaps they were well suited to do when we first heard or made use of them. When we continually tread one constant road of sentences or track of expressions, they become like an old beaten path which we daily travel and walk on without particularly noticing the parts along the way; so in our daily repetition of a form, we neglect due attention to the full sense of the words.

But there is something more suited to awaken the attention of the mind in a conceived prayer, when a Christian is making his own way toward God according to the present inclination of his soul and the urgency of his present wants. To use the words of a writer lately cited, 'While we are clothing the sense of our hearts in fit expressions and, as it were, digging the content of our prayers out of our own feelings and experiences, it must needs keep the heart closer at work.'

6. *The duty of prayer is very useful to reveal to us the frame of our own spirits.* But a constant use of forms will much hinder our knowledge of ourselves and prevent our acquaintance with our own hearts, which is one great spring of maintaining inward religion in its power. Daily observation of our own spirits would teach us where we are wanting and how to frame our prayers before God. But if we tie ourselves down to the same words always, our own observation of our hearts will be of little use, since we must speak the same expressions, whatever the frame of our hearts may be. Therefore, as an inward search of our souls and intimate acquaintance with ourselves is a means to obtain the gift of prayer, so the exercise of the gift of prayer will promote this self-acquaintance, which is discouraged and hindered by the restraint of forms.

Lastly, I mention the most usual, most evident and convincing argument against perpetual confinement of ourselves to a form. That is, because it renders our converse with God very imperfect. For it is not possible that forms of prayer should be composed that are perfectly suited to all our frames of spirit and fitted to all our occasions in the things of this life and the life to come. Our circumstances are always altering in this frail and mutable state. We have new sins to be confessed, new temptations and sorrows to be represented, new needs to be supplied. Every change of providence in the affairs of a nation, a family, or a person, requires suitable petitions and acknowledgements. No prescribed composition can ever provide well for all of these.

I confess, all our concerns of soul and body may be included in some large and general words of a form, which is no more suited to one time, place or condition than to another. But generalities are cold and do not affect us, or persons that join with us, or the one whose case should be represented before God. It is much sweeter to our own souls and to those of our fellow worshippers to have our fears, doubts, complaints, temptations and sorrows represented in most exact and particular expressions, in such language as the soul itself feels when the words are spoken.

Now, though we should often meet with prayers pre-composed that are fitted to express our present case, the gift of prayer is much better than any form, just as a general skill in the work of preaching is to be preferred to any pre-composed sermons; as a perfect knowledge in the art of medical practice is better than any number of recipes; or as a recipe to make a medicine is preferable to one single medicine already made. He who binds himself always to read printed sermons will not arrive at the art of preaching; and the man who deals only in recipes shall never become a skilful physician; nor can the gift of prayer be attained by everlasting confinement to forms.

Perhaps it may make stronger impressions on some persons, and go further towards the cure of confinement to forms and prejudices against the gift of prayer, to hear what a bishop of the Church of England has said on this matter:

'In the use of such prescript forms to which a man has been accustomed, he ought to be narrowly watchful over his own heart, for fear of that lip-service and formality which in such cases we are more especially exposed to. For anyone to set down and satisfy himself with his book-prayer, or some prescript form, and to go no further, is still to remain in his infancy and not to grow up in his new nature. This would be as if a man who once had need of crutches should always afterwards make use of them, and so necessitate himself to a continual impotency. Prayer by book is commonly of itself something flat and dead, floating for the most part too much in generalities, and not particular enough for each occasion. There is not that life and vigour in it to engage the affections as when it proceeds immediately from the soul itself and is the natural expression of those particulars of which we are most sensitive. It is not easy to express what a vast difference a man may find, in respect of inward comfort and satisfaction, between those private prayers that are thus conceived from the affections, and those prescribed forms which we say by rote or read out of books' (Bishop Wilkins in his *Gift of Prayer*).

2. Another extreme to be avoided is a neglect of preparation for prayer and an entire dependence on sudden motions and suggestions: as though we were to expect the perpetual impression of the Holy Spirit upon our minds as upon the minds of the apostles and inspired saints; as though we had reason to hope for his continual impulses in the content, manner and words of prayer, without any forethought, care or premeditation of our own.

It is true indeed that when a man has premeditated the content and method of his prayer ever so exactly, he ought not to confine himself so as to neglect or check any warm and pious desires that may arise in his heart in the midst of the duty. But this does not hinder. It is lawful and proper by all useful means to endeavour in general to learn the holy skill of praying and to prepare also by meditation, or reading, or holy conversation, for the particular exercise of this gift and the performance of this duty.

Some persons imagine that if they use no form, they must always pray extempore, or without any premeditation, and are ready to think that all free or conceived prayer is extemporary. But these things ought to be distinguished.

Conceived or free prayer is when the words of our prayer are not formed beforehand to direct our thoughts, but we conceive the matter of substance of our addresses to God first in our minds, and then put those conceptions into such words and expressions as we think most proper. This may be done by some work of meditation before we begin to speak in prayer, partly with regard to the thoughts, and partly the expressions, too.

Extemporary prayer is when, without any reflection or meditation beforehand, we address ourselves to God and speak the thoughts of our hearts as fast as we conceive them. This is most properly done in what is called ejaculatory prayer, when we lift up our souls to God in short breathings of request or thanksgiving in the midst of any common affairs of life. But there may be also some other occasions for it:

i. I grant that in secret prayer, the same degree of premeditation is not necessary, as in public. For there a person takes a greater liberty to express his thoughts and the desires of his soul just as they rise within him, which may be very significant to awaken and maintain his own affections in that duty, though perhaps they would be very improper and disagreeable in public.

ii. I grant also that persons of better natural abilities, of a lively temperament or ready expression, of great heavenly-mindedness, or such as have been long exercised and experienced in this work, are not bound to premeditate all the materials and method of their prayer in daily worship in a family. Nor are ministers, whose graces and talents have been well developed, obliged to think over all the substance of every public address to God beforehand. A short recollection of thought may supply such persons with content for those constant returns of worship. Nor are Christians who are possessed of such endowments at any time bound to an equal degree of premeditation as others are. Bishop Wilkins very pertinently tells us, 'The proportion of gifts that a man has received is the measure of his work and duty in this case.' Yet upon some great and solemn occasions, public and private, when times are set apart for prayer, a regular premeditation is very useful and advantageous to persons of the highest attainments.

iii. I grant further that there may be calls of providence which may demand sudden addresses to God even from persons of less skill and experience; and they have reason to hope for more special assistance from the Spirit of God while they obey the call of present and necessary duty.

But I am ready to suspect that some persons who are unskilled in praying and yet cry out against premeditation indulge a degree of secret spiritual sloth while they profess to be afraid of anything that comes near to a form.

The arguments that may incline and encourage younger Christians to prepare their thoughts for prayer beforehand are these:

1. The common reason of man and the light of nature teach us that an affair of such solemnity and importance, which requires our utmost care to perform it well, cannot be done without some forethought. The skill of a Christian in the inward exercise of grace is to be learned and improved by forethought and diligence; much more in the external performance of a religious duty. Now if the light of nature leads us to it, and Scripture nowhere forbids, why should we not pursue the practice? The words of Scripture seem to encourage such a premeditation, when they tell us we should not be rash with our mouth nor let our heart be hasty to utter anything before God (*Eccles.* 5:2).

2. That the heart should be prepared for prayer is certainly necessary; the preparation of the heart is frequently spoken of in the Word of God. But the heart cannot be prepared for any act of worship without some degree of premeditation. What is the use of reading the Word of God just before prayer in our families? Why are we so often advised to recollect the sermons we hear when we retire for prayer, but that by premeditation we may be better fitted with material for this duty?

3. There can be no such thing as learning to pray in a regular way without it. The division of the nature of prayer into several parts – adoration, confession, petition – is all useless if we must not think beforehand. The excellent rules that ministers lay down to teach us to pray are mere trifling if we must not think beforehand. If we may not consider what our sins are, what our wants are, and what our mercies are before we speak in prayer, there is no possibility of ever learning to perform this part of Christian worship with any tolerable measure of decency or profit. An utter aversion to thinking beforehand,

whatever the reasons, will be a most effectual bar against the attainment of the gift of prayer in any considerable degree.

4. Due preparation for prayer is the way to serve God with our best. For younger Christians unskilled in this work to rush always into the presence of God in solemn prayer without due forethought even when there is time allowed for it, and to pour out words before God at all adventures, is no sign of that high reverence which they owe to so awesome a majesty, before whom angels veil their faces, and who is jealous of his own worship and abhors the sacrifice of fools.

If we utterly neglect preparation, we shall be ready to fall into many difficulties. Sometimes we shall be constrained to make long and indecent stops in prayer, not knowing what to say next. At other times we shall be in danger of saying things that are very little to the point, and of wandering far from our purposed subject and design, which can never be acceptable to God. And sometimes when the mind is not regularly equipped, we run into a confused, incoherent and impertinent rhapsody of words, by which both God may be dishonoured, and the edification of ourselves and others spoiled. The Spirit of God stands afar off from us for a season; perhaps for the purpose of reproving our negligence of a wise and holy care to learn to pray.

Some unhappy practices such as these in the last age have given great offence to the pious and have been a stumbling-block and scandal to the profane. The wicked and profane world have taken the occasion to throw loads of reproach on all conceived prayer, under the name of praying extempore, and have endeavoured to render all prayer without books and forms as odious as possible under this name. The more sober and pious part of the Church of England, which usually worship God by liturgies and pre-composed forms, have been too ready to give ear to these reproaches and have by this means been confirmed in their confinement to liturgies and prayer-books. They have been hardened against attempting to seek the gift of prayer themselves and have been tempted to oppose and censure those who have attained it. No small share of this public scandal will be found at the door of those few bold, ignorant and careless men who have been guilty of such rash and thoughtless addresses to God, under a pretence of praying by the Spirit.

In opposition to this practice of premeditation, some pious and sincere Christian may say, 'I have now and then meditated many things which I intended to speak in prayer; but when I came to pray, I have found my thoughts enlarged beyond all my preparations and carried away to dwell in prayer upon subjects and petitions of a very different kind, and in a much more lively manner to express my thoughts than I had before conceived.' Now I would persuade such a person to receive this divine assistance, not as an argument to neglect premeditation for the future, but as a reward of his diligence in preparing his heart beforehand for this work.

Another Christian will tell me that sometimes when he has thought over many materials for his prayer before, he has found a greater confusion in his mind between his former preparations and his present suggestions than if he prayed in an extemporary way. In reply to this objection, I must confess that I have sometimes had the same unhappy experience: but I impute it to one of these three defects:

Either my premeditation was very slight and imperfect as to the content or method, so that I had not arranged the subjects of my prayer in any settled form and order in my memory, but left them almost as much in uncertainty as new thoughts that might occur to my mind in praying. And it is more troublesome sometimes to mend and finish what is very imperfect than to make entirely new.

Or perhaps my premeditation had been chiefly the work of my head, without so due a consultation of the frame of my heart. I had prepared my head but not my heart for prayer. And then it is no wonder that when the heart comes to be warmly engaged in praying it runs far away from the mere premeditations of the head, and sometimes between both they create a confusion in the mind.

Or it may be that my soul has been out of frame and indisposed for prayer, and then I would not lay the fault upon premeditation; the prayer would have been as bad or worse without it.

But where my preparation both of head and heart has been carefully and wisely managed, I have had several experiences of the convenience and usefulness of it, especially in my younger years, and upon some extraordinary and solemn occasions.

Finally, if some persons have conscientiously and with due diligence attempted this way, and find they always pray more usefully and more honourably, with more regularity and delight, by the mere preparation of the heart for this duty, without fixing the parts and method of their prayer in their memory beforehand, they must follow those methods of devotion which they have found most effectual to attain the best ends. But they must not forbid the use of premeditation to others, whom God has owned and approved in that way.

And let it be observed that few Christians attain so great a readiness and regularity in the gift of prayer without learning by premeditation. Far greater is the number of those whose performances are mediocre, for want of thinking beforehand.

The Content of Prayer

FIRST, IT IS NECESSARY to furnish ourselves with proper content, that we may be able to hold much converse with God; to occupy our souls and others agreeably and devoutly in worship; to assist the exercise of our own graces and those of others by a rich supply of divine thoughts and desires in prayer; that we may not be forced to make too long and indecent pauses whilst we are performing that duty, nor break off abruptly as soon as we have begun, for want of content, nor pour out abundance of words to dress up narrow and scanty sense, for want of variety of devout thoughts.

I shall, therefore, first propose some rules in order to furnish ourselves with proper content for prayer, and then lay down some directions concerning these materials of prayer with which our souls are furnished.

RULES TO FURNISH US WITH CONTENT are these:

RULE 1: *Strive for a large acquaintance with all things that belong to religion, for there is nothing that relates to religion but may properly make some part of the content of our prayer.*

This is therefore the most general advice and the most universal rule that can be given in this case. Let us daily seek after a more extensive and a more affecting knowledge of God and of ourselves. A great acquaintance with God in his nature, in his persons, in his perfection, in his works and in his Word will supply us with abundant furniture for invocation, adoration, praise, thanksgiving and blessing; and will suggest to us many arguments in pleading with God for mercy. An intimate acquaintance with ourselves and a lively sense of our own frames of spirit, our needs, our sorrows and our joys will also supply us with proper thoughts for confession, for petition and for giving thanks. We should acquaint ourselves therefore with the Word of God in a great degree, for it is there he reveals himself to us and there he reveals us also to ourselves. Let the word of Christ dwell richly in you in all wisdom, that you may be furnished with petitions and praises.

We should also be watchful observers of the dealings of God with us in every ordinance and in every providence, and know well the state of our souls. We should observe the working of our hearts toward God and towards the creature, call ourselves to account often, and often examine our temper and our life in our natural, our civil and our religious actions. For this purpose, as well as upon many other accounts, it will be of great advantage to keep in writing some of the most remarkable providences of God and instances of his anger or mercy towards us, as well as some of our most remarkable carriages towards him, whether sins, or duties, or the exercises of grace. Such observations and remarks in our daily walking with God will be a growing treasury to furnish us for petition and praise. This seems to be the meaning of those Scriptures in which we read of watching unto prayer (*Eph.* 6:18, *1 Pet.* 4:7). This will make us always ready to say something to God in prayer, concerning both him and ourselves. Let our judgements be constantly well stored and our graces and affections be lively and lead us to the duty;

for the most part some proper content will naturally arise and flow with ease and pleasure.

> RULE 2: *Let the nature of this duty of prayer, as divided into its several parts, be impressed upon our hearts and dwell in our memories.*

Let us always remember that it contains in it these several parts of worship, namely, invocation, adoration, confession, petition, pleading, profession (or self-resignation), thanksgiving, and blessing. That we may retain them better in our minds, they may be summed up in these four lines:

> Call upon God, adore, confess,
> Petition, plead, and then declare
> You are the Lord's, give thanks and bless,
> And let *Amen* confirm the prayer.

And by a recollection of these several parts of prayer, we may be assisted to go on step by step, and to improve in the gift of performance of this part of worship.

It would tend also to develop the gift of prayer if persons who have time and capacity would set down in writing all these parts of prayer as commonplaces, and all the observable passages that occur in reading the Holy Scripture or other authors. Or such passages as we hear delivered in prayer that are very affecting to our souls should be written down and registered under those heads. This would preserve in our memories the thoughts and expressions which have had a peculiar quickening influence upon us. Bishop Wilkins, in his *Treatise of Prayer*, has given us such collections of Scripture; and Mr Henry, in a recent book, has furnished us with a great many more, judiciously arranged under their proper subjects.

RULE 3. *If you wish to be furnished with larger supplies of material, do not content yourselves merely with generalities, but go into particulars in your confessions, petitions and thanksgiving.*

Enter into a particular consideration of the attributes, the glories, the graces and the relations of God. Express your sins, your wants and your sorrows, with a particular sense of the mournful circumstances that attend them. It will enlarge your hearts with prayer and humiliation if you confess the aggravations that increase the guilt of your sins, namely, whether they have been committed against knowledge, against the warnings of conscience, etc. It will furnish you with large matter for thankfulness if you run over the exalting and heightening circumstances of your mercies and comforts, namely, that they are great, spiritual and eternal, as well as temporal; that they were granted before you sought them, or as soon as asked, etc. And let your petitions and your thanksgiving in a special manner be suited to the place and circumstances of yourselves, those that you pray with, and those that you pray for.

Our burdens, our cares, our wants and our sins are many; so are our mercies, and our hopes; so are the attributes of our God, his promises and his graces. If we open our mouths wide, he will fill and satisfy us with good things, according to his Word. If generalities were sufficient for us, one short form would make all others needless. It would be enough to express ourselves to God in this manner: 'O Lord, thou art great and good, but we are vile sinners. Give us all the mercies we stand in need of for time and for eternity, for the sake of Jesus Christ; and through him accept all our thanksgivings for whatever we have and hope for. To the Father, Son and Holy Spirit, be eternal glory. Amen.'

This is a most general and comprehensive prayer and includes in it everything necessary. But no Christian can satisfy his soul, or go from day to day to the mercy-seat, and say nothing else but this. A saint in a right frame loves to pour out his soul before God in a hundred particulars, and God expects his children to feel affected with their own special wants and his peculiar mercies, and to take notice of the lesser as well as of the more considerable circumstances of them. Let us not be confined in ourselves then, for the hand of God and his heart are not confined. Our Lord Jesus bids us ask, and promises it shall be given (*Matt.* 7:7). The Apostle Paul bids us in everything by prayer and supplication to make known our requests to God (*Phil.* 4:6). And the Apostle James tells us that we receive not, because we ask not (*James* 4:2).

RULE 4: *In order to furnish our minds with content for prayer, it is very convenient at solemn times of worship to read some part of the Word of God, or some spiritual treatise written by holy men; or to converse with fellow Christians about divine things; or to spend some time in recollection or meditation of things that belong to religion.*

This will not only supply us with divine content, but will compose our thoughts in solemnity. Just before we engage in that work, we should be absent a little from the world, that our spirits may be freer for converse with God. We may borrow content for prayer from the word which we read, from inward reflections of our own souls, or from holy conferences. Many a saint has found it true that while he mused the fire burned within him (*Psa.* 39:3). And while we speak to men about the affairs of religion and inward piety, we shall certainly find something to say to God.

RULE 5: *If after all we find our hearts very barren and hardly know how to frame a prayer before God of ourselves, it has often been useful to take a book in our hand which contains some spiritual meditations in a petitionary form, some devout reflections or excellent patterns of prayer: above all, the psalms of David, some of the prophecies of Isaiah, some chapters in the Gospels, or any of the Epistles.*

Thus we may lift up our hearts to God in secret in short requests, adoration or thanksgiving, according as the verses or paragraphs we read are suited to the case of our own souls. This has obtained the name of mixed prayer (of which there is a further account under the fifth head of the last chapter).

Many Christians have experienced as a very agreeable help and of great advantage in their private devotions that when they could not of themselves speak a prayer to God, they could yet intersperse what they read with holy breathings toward God with fervent petitions. By this means they have found their souls warmed, and often in the sight of God have performed this duty more agreeably in this method than other persons of a larger and more extensive gift, with greater supplies of material, and much fluency of language. Nor can I disapprove of what Bishop Wilkins says concerning secret prayer, namely, 'That it is not always necessary here that a man should still keep on in a continued frame of speech; but in private devotions a man may take a greater freedom both for his phrase and content. He may sometimes be at a standstill and make a pause; there may be intermissions and blank spaces, in which by meditation he may recover new content to continue in this duty.'

RULE 6: *If you find your heart so very dry and unaffected with the things of religion that you can say nothing at all to God in prayer, that no divine content occurs to your thoughts, go and fall down humbly before God and tell him with a grievous complaint that you can say nothing to him, that you can do nothing but groan and cry before him. Go and tell him that without his Spirit you cannot speak one expression, that without immediate assistance from his grace you cannot proceed in this worship. Tell him humbly that he must lose a morning or an evening sacrifice if he does not condescend to send down fire from heaven upon the altar.*

Plead with him earnestly for his own Spirit, even if only in the language of sighs and tears. Beg that he would never suffer your heart to be so hard, nor your soul to be so empty of divine things, that he would not only now, but at all times, supply you for so glorious a work as this converse with himself. God knows the mind of his own Spirit, and he hears those groanings that cannot be uttered, and he understands their language when the soul is, as it were, imprisoned and shut up that it cannot vent itself. Our heavenly Father hears the groans of the prisoner (*Psa.* 102:20). And there has been glorious communion maintained with God before the end of that time of worship, when at the beginning of it the saint could say nothing else but, 'Lord, I cannot pray.'

Let it be noted here that when there is such a heaviness and deadness upon the spirit, such a coldness or distraction in this worship and such an averseness and reluctance in the mind, it ought to be a matter of humiliation and deep self-abasement before God, especially whenever we sense that it is owing to our own negligence or to some recent guilt brought upon the conscience. Earnestly we should beg pardon for it; and as Bishop Wilkins says, 'What we lack in the degrees of our duty, we should be sure to make up in humility; and this will be the most proper use of our failings, when we can strengthen ourselves by our very infirmities.'

I now lay down some directions concerning the content of our prayers, how to manage it aright.

DIRECTION 1: *Do not think it absolutely necessary to insist upon all the parts of prayer in every address to God, though in our stated and solemn prayers there are but few that can be well left out. What we omit at one time we may perhaps pursue at another with more lively affection, so that we may fulfil all our errands at the throne of grace.*

But let us be sure to insist most upon those things which are warmest in our own hearts, especially in secret. This is a good advice even in social prayers, when those things with which we are deeply affected concern the company that joins with us. Also, let the parts of prayer have the largest share in the performance, for which our spirit is best prepared and with which it is most sensibly impressed at the present time; whether it be adoration, petition, confession or thanksgiving. This will not only supply us with material, but will keep our spirits lively in the work and will be the best means to affect those that join with us and to call their graces into exercise. Those things indeed which our fellow worshippers cannot be concerned in are better laid aside till we come to speak to God alone.

DIRECTION 2: *Suit the subject of your prayer to the special occasion of each particular duty, to the circumstances of the*

*time, place and persons with, and for whom, you pray. This
will be another source of material and will direct you to
the choice of proper thoughts and language for every part
of prayer.*

i. *The time.* If it is morning, we may adore God as the
watchful shepherd of Israel who slumbers not, nor sleeps.
Then we confess our inability to have defended ourselves
through all the hours of darkness, while nature and our
active powers lie, as it were, useless and dead. Then we
give thanks to him that he has secured us from the spirits
of darkness, given us rest in measure, and raised us in
peace, 'I laid me down and slept; I awaked; for the Lord
sustained me' (*Psa.* 3:5). Then we petition for divine
counsel in all the affairs of the day, and the presence of
God with us through all its cares, businesses, dangers and
duties.

In the evening we give thanks to God for the mercies
of the day for which we offered our petitions in the
morning: We confess the sins and follies of the day and
humble our souls before God. We petition for proper
mercies the succeeding night, with expressions of
adoration, confession and self-resignation, suited to the
time, 'I will both lay me down in peace, and sleep: for
thou, O Lord, only makest me dwell in safety' (*Psa.* 4:8).

Thus when we pray before or after a meal; on the Lord's
Day or our common days of business; in a time of war or
peace; in a time of public or private rejoicing; on a day of
trouble or humiliation. Let the several expressions of our
prayer, in the various parts of it, be suited to the particular
time.

ii. *The place and the persons.* In our secret devotions, we
may adore God in this language: 'O Lord God, who seest

in secret, who knowest the way that I take, thou hast commanded that thy children should seek thee in their closets, and thou hast promised to reward them openly.' Here also we ought to confess our more particular sins which the world does not know, and pour out our whole souls before God with great freedom and plainness. We tell him all our follies, our infirmities, our joys and sorrows, our brightest hopes, our most gloomy and dismal fears, and all the inward workings of our hearts, either towards himself or towards others. We converse with God aright in prayer when we, as it were, maintain a divine friendship with him in secret, and in our humble addresses communicate with him as our heavenly and condescending friend.

When we pray in a family, the content must be suited to the circumstances of the household, in confession of family sins, petitions and thanksgiving for family mercies; whether those with whom we live are sick or in health; whether they are in distress or in peace; whether fixed in their habitations, or moving. Our language to God ought to be suited to this variety of conditions.

If we pray among a select society of Christians, we draw near to God with holy boldness, something like what we use in our duties of secret worship. We have reason to take more freedom among fellow saints and whose hearts have felt many of the same workings as our own. Then when our faith is lively, we should give thanks to God for our election in Christ Jesus, for the atonement and righteousness of the Son of God, in which we humbly hope to have an interest; for the enlightening and sanctifying work of his own Spirit upon our hearts; for our expectations of eternal glory. By expressing the joys of our faith to God, we may often be made a means, in the hands of the Holy Spirit, to raise the faith and joy of others.

In public worship or in family devotions, where saints and sinners are present, a minister or a Christian who speaks in prayer should consider the circumstances of the whole congregation or family, and plead for suitable mercies. But I do not think he should be ashamed to express his faith and hope when he speaks to God, where there are many to join with him in that holy language, though not every single hearer can heartily join and consent. Perhaps this may be a way to make unconverted persons that are present blush and be ashamed and be inwardly grieved that they are forced to leave out many of the expressions of prayer used by the minister, and are convinced in themselves, and confounded, because they cannot join in the same language of faith and hope, joy and thankfulness. For it is not necessary that every worshipper should lift up his soul to God according to every sentence spoken in social prayer, but only to such as are suited to his own case and state, and such as he can sincerely speak to God himself.

DIRECTION 3: *Do not affect to pray long, for the sake of length, or to stretch out your subjects by labour and toil of thought, beyond the reserves of your own spirit.*

God is not the more pleased with prayers merely because they are long, nor are Christians ever the more edified. When we feel our spirits dry and our hearts constrained, it is much better to make up by the frequency of our devotions what they lack in length. We may also cry to God for the aids of his own Holy Spirit, even in the middle of our prayer, to carry us forward in that work.

But not everyone is fit to pray at length. God has bestowed a variety of natural, as well as spiritual talents and gifts upon men. Nor is the best Christian or a saint of the greatest gifts always fit for long prayers. For long prayers may lead to many difficulties. The difficulties of affected length in prayer are these.

i. Sometimes a person is betrayed by an affectation of long prayers into crude, rash and unseemly expressions in the presence of God. These are unworthy of his divine majesty and unbecoming of our baseness. Sometimes he is forced into irrelevant digressions and wanders away from the subject in hand till his thoughts again recover themselves; true spiritual worship is thereby hindered and corrupted. We shall rather take the advice of Solomon upon this account: 'Be not rash to utter any thing before God: for God is in heaven, and thou upon earth: therefore let thy words be few' (*Eccles.* 5:2).

ii. We are tempted to tautologies, to say the same things over and over again, which our Saviour highly blames. 'When ye pray, use not vain repetitions as the heathen do: for they think that they shall be heard for their much speaking' (*Matt.* 6:7). Sometimes, indeed, in the midst of our warm affections in prayer, we are delightfully constrained to a repetition of the same words through mere fervency of spirit, and there are instances of this in Scripture. But for the most part our repetitions are evidence not of the fervency, but of the barrenness of our minds and the slightness of our frame.

iii. Again, we shall be in danger, through an affectation of length, of tiring those that join with us, especially when a prayer is drawn out to many words, with much dullness and deadness of spirit and without an agreeable variety of thought. I confess, when the Spirit is poured in plentiful degrees upon men, and upon some extraordinary occasions, persons have continued for an hour or two together, with a delightful variety of content and expression; and instead of toil and labour to hold on, they found it difficult to break off. Their souls have been all the while near to God, and they have held the attention of those that joined with them, and kept their devotion warm. Our fathers have seen and felt it. But that spirit is much departed in our day, and there are seldom found amongst us any great lengths of prayer with equal affection and devotion, maintained either in ourselves or others, through so long a duty.

iv. We are tempted also sometimes by this means to exceed the time allotted for us in prayer, especially where others are to succeed in the same work. Or else we may encroach upon other parts of worship that are to follow, and some of our fellow worshippers are made uneasy. And when persons are under a necessary engagement to be elsewhere by an appointed time, or to be engaged in other duties, the latter part of their devotion is generally spoiled. It may be remarked here that even when Jacob wrestled with the angel, he was required to let him go, for it was break of day (*Gen.* 32:26). As we must not allow one duty to crowd out another, neither should we manage any duty so as to make it a hard task to ourselves or a toil to others, but a pleasure and spiritual occupation to both.

v. I might add, lastly, that by this excessive affectation of length in prayer without an equal degree of the spirit of prayer and lively devotion, some imprudent Christians have given too much occasion to the profane scoffers of the age. The wicked of the earth have among themselves rendered these methods of converse with God ridiculous and have reproached the gift and spirit of prayer because of our irregular performance of that part of worship. Whereas when the Spirit of God, by his own immediate and uncommon influences draws out the heart to continue in prayer, these difficulties will not follow. While I am discouraging young Christians from the affectation of long prayers which arises from ostentation of their parts, or from a superstitious hope of pleasing God better by saying many words, or from a trifling frame of spirit, I would not have my readers imagine that the shortest prayers are always the best.

Our sinful natures are too ready to put off God in secret or in the family with a few minutes of worship from mere sloth and weariness of holy things, which is equally to be blamed. For we thereby omit a great part of the necessary work of prayer in confessions, petitions, pleadings for mercy, or thanksgiving.

Nor do I think that prayer in public assemblies should be so short, as though its only purpose were a mere preface before the sermon or a benediction after it. Social prayer is one considerable part, if not the chief duty, of public worship; and we ought generally to continue in it long enough to run through the most necessary and important purposes of a social address to the throne of grace. Christian prudence will teach us to determine the length of our prayers according to the occasion and present circumstances, and according to the measure of our own ability for this work.

The Method of Prayer

METHOD IS NECESSARY to guide our thoughts, to regulate our expressions and to arrange the several parts of prayer in such an order as is most easily understood by those who join with us, and most proper to inspire and maintain our own devotion and theirs. Though the same just and exact regularity is not necessary here as in preaching the Word, a well regulated prayer is most agreeable to men, honourable in the sight of the world, and not at all the less pleasing to God. The Spirit of God, when he is poured out as a spirit of prayer in the most glorious measures, does not contradict the rules of a natural and reasonable method, although his methods may have infinite variety in them.

Some method must be used in order to protect us from confusion, so that our thoughts are not ill sorted, or mingled and huddled together in a tumultuous and unseemly manner. It will be of use to prevent tautologies or repetitions, when each part of prayer is arranged in its proper place. It will guard us against roving digressions, when we have arranged our thoughts into order through-out every step of our prayer. We can judge what sort of subject properly and naturally follows what we are at present speaking, so that there is no need to fill up any empty spaces with content that is not proper or not suited to the purpose. Persons who profess to pray without observing any method at all, if they are very acceptable and affecting to others in their gift, do certainly use a secret and a natural method and properly connect one thing with another, though they themselves have not laid down any rule to themselves for it nor take notice of the order of their own prayers.

The general rules of method in prayer, which I would recommend to you, are these three.

RULE 1: *Let the general and the specific subjects in prayer be well distinguished, and usually let generalities be mentioned first with specifics following.*

For example, in adoration we acknowledge that God is all over glorious in his nature, self-sufficient and all sufficient, and we mention this with the deepest reverence and universal abasement of soul; and then we descend to praise him for his particular attributes of power, wisdom, goodness, etc., and exercise our particular graces accordingly. So in confession: we first acknowledge ourselves vile sinners, corrupt by nature, and of the same sinful mass with the rest of mankind; and then we confess our particular iniquities and our special guilt. So in our petitions: we pray first for the churches of Christ all over the world and his interest and his gospel throughout the earth; and then we petition for the churches in this nation, in this city, or that particular church of Christ to which we belong.

Sometimes, indeed, there is a beauty also in summing up all the particulars lastly in one generality, as when we have praised God for his many perfections to the utmost of our capacity, and we cry out, 'Lord, thou art exalted above all our praises; thou art altogether great and glorious.' Or when we have confessed several particular sins, we fall down before God as persons that are all over defiled and guilty. When we have petitioned for particular mercies, we then ask that God, who is able to do for us above what we can ask or think, would bestow all other comforts and every blessing that he knows needful for us. But still this rule must be observed, that general and particular heads ought to be so distinguished as to make our method of prayer natural and agreeable.

RULE 2: *Let things of the same kind, for the most part, be put together in prayer.*

We should not run from one part to another by starts and sudden wild thoughts and then return often to the same part again, going backward and forward in confusion. This bewilders the mind of him that prays, disgusts our fellow worshippers and injures their devotion. This will lead us into vain repetitions, and we shall lose ourselves in the work.

Yet I would make this exception. Sometimes the same matter may come naturally under two or three parts of prayer and be properly mentioned in two or three places by a judicious worshipper. We may mention some of the attributes of God under the head of adoration, where we praise him for his own perfections, and again under the head of pleading for mercy, when we use his power, his wisdom, or his goodness as an argument to enforce our petitions. We may mention his attributes under the head of thanksgiving also, when we bless him for the benefits that proceed from his goodness, his power, or his wisdom. So, in the beginning of a prayer, in our invocation of God, we put in a sentence or two of confession of our un-worthiness and of petition for divine assistance; and towards the conclusion of prayer it is not amiss to use a sentence or two consisting of such matter as may leave a suitable impression upon our minds, though perhaps something of the same matter may have been mentioned before.

For example, we may ask forgiveness of all the imperfections of our holy things; entreat that God would hear all our requests in the name of our Lord Jesus; recommend our prayers into the hands of our Redeemer, our great High Priest; and commit our whole selves to the conduct of divine grace, till we are brought safe to glory. But all this must be done with such a variety of expression, and proper connections, that it will be agreeable in itself, and occupy the minds of those that join with us, giving them delight rather than hindering their devotion.

RULE 3: *In every part of prayer, let those things which are the proper objects of our judgement be first mentioned, and then those that influence and move our affections.*

I do not mean that we should follow a manner of prayer that is more like preaching, as some imprudently have done, speaking many divine truths without the form or air of prayer. That is a very improper custom which some persons have taken up and indulged; when divine truths come to be mentioned in prayer, they run at great lengths in a doctrinal way. Yet there is frequently occasion in prayer, under its several parts, for recollecting divine truths, and these lay a proper foundation for warm and heartfelt expressions to follow, as, 'O Lord, thou art good, and thou dost good; why should I continue so long without partaking of thy goodness? My sins are great, and my iniquities have many aggravations. O that I might mourn for them before thee in secret! O that I could pour out my soul before thee in sorrow because of multiplied offences!' Thus let the language of emotion follow the language of our judgement, for this is the most rational and natural method.

HAVING LAID DOWN these general rules, the best particular method I can direct you to is that division of the parts of prayer mentioned in the foregoing chapter. I do not know a more natural order of things than this. To begin with invocation, or calling upon God, then to proceed to adore that God whom we invoke because of his various glories, we are then naturally led to confession, considering what little contemptible creatures we are in the presence of a God to be so adored, and to humbling ourselves because of our abounding sins and our many necessities. When we have given praise to a God of such holiness and have spread our wants before him, petitions for mercy naturally follow, and our requests should be accompanied by pleading with such divine arguments as the Spirit and the Word of God put into our mouths. Lastly we resign ourselves into the hands of God and express our self-dedication to him. Then we recall the mercies we have received, and out of gratitude pay him our tribute of honour and thanks. And as he is glorious in himself, and glorious in his works of power and grace, so we bless him and ascribe everlasting glory to him.

I cannot but think it a very useful thing for young beginners in the work of prayer to remember all these heads in their order and to express their thoughts and desires before God in this method, proceeding regularly from one part to another. And as this must be useful to assist and teach us to pray in public, so sometimes in our secret devotions it may not be improper to pursue the same practice.

Yet, it must be granted, there is no necessity of confining ourselves to a form in prayer. Sometimes the mind is so divinely full of one particular part of prayer, perhaps of thanksgiving, or of self-resignation, that high expressions of gratitude and of devoting ourselves to God break out first: 'Lord, I am come to devote myself to thee in an everlasting covenant; I am thine through thy grace, and through thy grace I will be thine for ever.' Or: 'Blessed be thy name, O Lord God Almighty, for thine abundant benefits that fill my soul with the sense of them; for thou hast pardoned all my iniquities and healed all my diseases.'

Sometimes, even in the beginning of a prayer, when we are insisting on one of the first parts of it, we receive a divine hint from the Spirit of God that carries away our thoughts and our whole souls with warm devotion into another part that is of a very different kind and perhaps usually comes in near the conclusion. And when the Spirit of God thus leads us, and our souls are in a very devout frame, we are not to quench the Spirit of God in order to tie ourselves to any set rules of prescribed method.

It is not necessary that persons of great talents, of divine affections, of much converse with God, and that have attained a good degree of this gift by long exercise, should bind themselves to any one certain method of prayer. For we find the prayers recorded in Holy Scripture very diverse in their order and disposition, as the Spirit of God and the divine affections of those saints led and guided them. But still there is some method observed, and it may be traced and demonstrated.

I am persuaded that if young Christians did not give themselves up in their first efforts at prayer to a loose and negligent habit of speaking everything that comes uppermost, but attempted to learn this holy skill by recollecting the several parts of prayer and expressing their thoughts in this method, great numbers in our churches would have arrived at a good degree of the gift of prayer and be capable afterwards of giving a more glorious and unbounded liberty to their souls, without breaking the rules of just and natural method – and that to the great edification of our churches as well as of their own families.

Expression in Prayer

Prayer is the proper work of the heart; yet in this present state, in secret as well as in social prayer, the language of the lips is an excellent aid in this part of worship.

A person indeed may pray heartily and effectually and yet make use of no words. Sometimes the desires of the heart may be too big to be expressed, when the Spirit of

God is with us in plentiful operations and assists us to plead with sighs and groans which cannot be uttered (*Rom.* 8:26). Persons that are mute may think over their wants and raise their souls to God in longing desires and wishes for grace in a time of need. Nor is it necessary of using language upon God's account, for he knows the desires of our heart and our most secret breathings towards him. He that hears without ears understands us without our words. Yet as language is of absolute necessity in social prayer, that others may join with us in our addresses to God, so for the most part we find it necessary in secret, too, for there are few persons of so steady and fixed a power of meditation as to maintain warm devotion and to converse with God, or with themselves profitably, without words.

Expressions are useful not only to dress our thoughts, but sometimes to form and perfect the ideas and inclinations of our minds. The use of words makes us doubly conscious of the things we conceive. They serve to awaken the holy passions of the soul as well as to express them. Our expressions sometimes follow and reveal the warmer stirrings of the heart; and sometimes they are dictated by the judgement and are a means to warm the heart and excite those holy motions. They fix and engage all our powers in religion and worship, and they serve to regulate as well as to increase our devotion. We are told to take with us words, and turn to the Lord and say to him, Take away all iniquity, and receive us graciously (*Hos.* 14:2). And in the psalms of David, we often read of his crying to the Lord with his voice and making supplication with his tongue, when the content of his prayer is such that we have abundant reason to believe that it was performed in secret.

Here I shall first lay down some directions how to attain a rich treasure of expression in prayer. And secondly I shall give several rules about the choice and use of words and expressions.

DIRECTION 1: *Besides the general acquaintance with God and with yourselves that was prescribed in a previous section, labour after the fresh, particular and lively sense of the greatness and grace of God, and of your own needs, sins and mercies, whenever you come to pray.*

This will supply you with an abundance of proper expressions. The passions of the mind, when they are moved, do mightily help the tongue. They fill the mouth with arguments. They give a natural eloquence to those who know no rules of art. And they almost constrain the dumb to speak. There is a remarkable instance of this in ancient history: when the son of Croesus the king, Atys, who was mute from his childhood, saw his father ready to be slain, the violence of his passion broke the bonds that tied his tongue and he cried out to save him. Beggars that have a pinching sense of hunger and cold find a variety of expressions to tell us their wants and to plead for relief. Let our spiritual senses therefore be always awake and lively and our affections always warm, and let them lead the duty; then words will follow in a greater or lesser degree.

DIRECTION 2: *Treasure up the expressions especially that you read in Scripture, and that you have found in other books of devotion or have heard fellow Christians make use of, by which your own hearts have been consciously moved and warmed.*

Those forms of speaking that have had great influence and success upon our feelings at one time may probably have a like effect also at other times – if we take care not to confine ourselves to them constantly, lest formality and thoughtlessness should grow.

Though the limiting ourselves to a constant set form of words is justly disapproved, serious, pious and well-composed patterns of prayer may yet be greatly used in order to form our expressions and furnish us with proper praying language. And I wish the assistances that might be borrowed from these were not as superstitiously abandoned by some persons as they are idolised by others. But I suppose no one will disapprove the advice, if I ask them to remember the more heartfelt sentences in the Psalms of David, and the complaints of Job, and other holy men, when they breathe out their souls to God in worship.

These in a nearer and more particular sense may be called the words which the Holy Spirit teaches, and whenever they suit our circumstances, they will always be pleasing to God. Moreover, they are such as Christians are most acquainted with and pious souls are most affected with. The Spirit of God in praying and preaching will often bless the use of his own language. And I am persuaded this is one way by which the Spirit helps our infirmities and becomes a Spirit of supplication in us, by suggesting to us particular passages of Scripture that are useful to furnish us with both content and expression in prayer.

The most authentic judge of fine thoughts and language that our age has produced assures us of the beauty and glory of the style of Scripture, and particularly in this respect, that it is most proper to teach us how to pray. I cannot refrain from transcribing this paragraph from the *Spectator*, June 14, 1712: Says he:

> It happens very well that the Hebrew idioms run into
> the English tongue with a peculiar grace and beauty:

our language has received innumerable elegancies and improvements from that infusion of hebraisms which are derived to it out of the poetical passages of Holy Writ; they give a force and energy to our expressions, warm and animate our language, and convey our thoughts in more ardent and intent phrases than any that are to be met with in our own tongue; there is something so passionate in this kind of diction that it often sets the mind in a flame and makes our hearts burn within us. How cold and dead does a prayer appear that is composed in the most elegant and polite forms of speech which are natural to our tongue, when it is not heightened by that solemnity of phrase which may be drawn from the sacred writings? It has been said by some of the ancients that if the gods were to talk with men, they would certainly speak in Plato's style; but I think we may say with justice, that when mortals converse with their creator, they cannot do it in so proper a style as that of the Holy Scriptures.

It would be of excellent use to improve us in the gift of prayer, if in our daily reading of the Word of God we observed what expressions were suited to the several parts of prayer – adoration, confession, petition or thanksgiving – and let them be used in our addresses to God that day. Indeed, if we remembered but one verse every day, and fixed it into our hearts by frequent meditation, and worked it into our prayers morning and evening, it would in time grow up to a treasure of divine meaning and language, fit to address our Maker upon all occurrences of life.

And it has been observed that persons of low capacity and no learning have attained to a good measure of this holy skill of prayer merely by having their minds well furnished with words of Scripture, and have been able to pour out their hearts before God in a fluency of proper thoughts and language, to the shame of those that have been blessed with brighter abilities and have enjoyed the advantage of a learned education.

Yet I would lay down two cautions about the use of Scripture language:

One is that we should not too much impose an allusive sense upon the words of Scripture, nor use them in our prayers in a sense very different from the true meaning of them. Not that I would utterly disallow and condemn all such allusive expressions, as, for instance, that which is frequently used when we desire mercies for our souls and bodies, to ask the blessings of the upper and the nether springs. There may be some such phrases used pertinently enough; the commonness of them also makes them somewhat more agreeable. Yet if we affect to show our wit or ingenuity by seeking pretty phrases of Scripture and using them in an allusive sense very foreign to the original purpose of them, we shall be in danger of leading ourselves into many mistakes in the interpretation of Scripture, and of exposing ourselves sometimes to the peril of mistaking the true sense of a text, by having frequently fixed a false meaning upon it in our prayers.

Another caution in using Scripture language is this: that we abstain from all those expressions which are of a very dubious sense and hard to be understood. If we indulge the use of such unclear sentences in our speaking to God, we might as well pray in an unknown tongue, which is so much disapproved by the apostle (*1 Cor.* 14:9, 14). Do not let the pomp and sound of any hard Hebrew names or obscure phrases in Scripture allure us to be fond of them in social prayer, even though we ourselves may know the meaning of them, lest we confound the thoughts of our fellow worshippers.

DIRECTION 3: *Be always ready to engage in holy conference and divine discourse.*

This will teach us to speak of the things of God. Let it be your delightful practice to recollect and talk over with one another the sermons you have heard, the books of divinity you have been conversant with, those parts of the Word of God you have lately read, and especially your own experience of divine things. By this you will gain a large treasure of language to clothe your pious thoughts and emotions.

It is a most profitable practice, after you have heard a sermon, to confer with some fellow Christian who also heard it, and run over all the particulars of it that you can retain in your memory. Then go away and pray them over again; that is, make them the content and substance of your address to God. Plead with him to instruct you in the truths that were mentioned; to incline you to perform the duties recommended and to mourn over and mortify the sins that were reproved; to teach you to trust and live upon the promises and comforts proposed, and to wait and hope for the glories revealed in that sermon. Let this be done frequently afterwards in the same week, if the sermon be suited to your case and condition of soul. This will furnish you incredibly with riches of content and expression for the great duty of prayer.

The reason we lack expressions in prayer is many times because we are so little used to speaking about the things of religion and another world. A man that has but a tolerable share of natural abilities, and no great fluency of speech, learns to talk well upon the affairs of his own trade and business in the world, and scarcely ever lacks words to discourse with his dealers. The reason is because his heart and his tongue are frequently engaged in them. Thus if our affections are kept warm and we become accustomed to speaking frequently of the things of religion to men, we shall learn to express ourselves much better about the same divine concerns when we come before God.

DIRECTION 4: *Pray earnestly for the gift of utterance, and seek the blessing of the Spirit of God upon the use of proper means to obtain a treasure of expressions for prayer.*

The great apostle prays often for a freedom of speech and utterance in his ministry, that he may speak the mystery of Christ and make it manifest so as he ought to speak (*Col.* 4:3, 4). So the gift of utterance in prayer is a very fit request to be made to God, for the advantage of our own souls and those that join with us. The wise man tells us that 'the preparation of the heart in man, and the answer of the tongue, is from the Lord' (*Prov.* 16:1). Let us pray then, that when God has prepared our heart for his worship, he would also teach our tongue to answer the thoughts and desires of the heart and to express them in words suitable and answering to all our inward spiritual feelings. A fitting variety of expression, and holy oratory in prayer, is one of these good and perfect gifts that come from above, from God, the Father of lights and knowledge (*James* 1:17).

THE RULES about the choice and use of proper expressions in prayer are these:

RULE 1: *Choose those expressions that best suit your meaning, that most exactly answer the ideas of your mind, and that are fitted to your sense and apprehension of things.*

For the design of prayer is to tell God the inward thoughts of your heart. If you speak what is not in the heart, though the words be ever so fine, it is but a mere mockery of God. Let your tongues be the true interpreters of your minds. When our souls are filled with a lively impression of some of the attributes or works of God, when our hearts are overpowered with a sense of our own guilt and unworthiness, or big with some important request, Oh what a blessed pleasure is it to hit upon a fitting expression that speaks our very soul and fulfils all our meaning! And what a pleasure does it convey to all that join with us, who have their spiritual senses exercised! And it helps to excite in them the same devotion that dictated to us the words we speak. The royal preacher sought out, and gave good heed to find and to set in order, acceptable words in his sermons, that they might be as goads and nails fastened by the master of assemblies (*Eccles.* 12:10–11); that is, that they might leave a strong and lasting impression on those who hear, that by piercing deep into the heart as goads, they might be fixed as nails. And there is the same reason for the choice of proper words in prayer.

RULE 2: *Use a way of speaking that may be most natural and easy to be understood and most agreeable to those that join with you.*

The apostle gives this direction to the Corinthians concerning their public worship; 'Except ye utter by the tongue words easy to be understood, how shall it be known what is spoken? for ye shall speak into the air' (*1 Cor.* 14:9). Avoid all foreign and uncommon words which are borrowed from other languages and not sufficiently familiar, or which are old and worn out of use.

Avoid those expressions which are too philosophical, and those which savour too much of mystical divinity. Avoid a long train of unclear metaphors, or of expressions that are used only by some particular violent faction. Avoid length and obscurity in your sentences and in the placing of your words, and do not intersperse your expressions with too many parentheses which cloud and entangle the sense.

And here I beg leave to give one or two instances of each of these improper methods of speaking; not that I ever heard these very phrases used by any ministers or private Christians in prayer. But as vices of the life are rendered most hateful and are best cured or prevented by seeing them represented in the plainest and most odious colours, so the vices of speech and improprieties of expression are best avoided by a plain representation of them in their own complete deformity.

This will deter us from coming near them and make us watchful against all those forms of speaking that border upon these follies. And indeed, without giving examples of each of these faults, I do not know how to make the unlearned Christian understand the thing he ought to avoid.

By uncommon words, I mean such as are either too old or too new for common use. Old and obsolete words and expressions are such as these: 'we do thee to wit' for 'we acquaint thee'; 'leasing' for 'lying'; 'a gin' for 'a snare'. Some such words as these yet stand in our translation of the Bible; many of these you may find in the old trans-lation of the Psalms in the *Book of Common Prayer* and in the metre of Hopkins and Sternhold. They were proper in the age when they were written but are now grown into contempt.

New words are for the most part borrowed from foreign languages, and should not be used in social prayer till they have grown so common that there appears no difficulty to the hearers nor affectation in the speaker. They might be such as these, which are of French origin: Thou, O Lord, art our *dernier resort* [that is, our *last refuge*]. The whole world is but one great machine managed by thy *puissance* [that is, an engine managed by thy *power*]. We are *chagrin*, because of the hurries and *tentations* of the *malign spirit* [that is, We are *vexed* and grow uneasy by reason of the *temptations* of the *devil*]. Or these, which are borrowed from the Latin: 'The beatific splendours of thy face irradiate the celestial region and felicitate the saints; there are the most exuberant profusions of thy grace, and the sempiternal efflux of thy glory.'

By philosophical expressions, I intend such as are taught in the academic schools in order to give learned men a shorter and more comprehensive view of things, or to distinguish nicely between ideas that are in danger of being mistaken without such distinction. As for instance, it is not proper to say to God in public prayer, 'Thou art hypostatically three, and essentially one. By the plenitude of perfection in thine essence, thou art self-sufficient for thine own existence and beatitude; who in an incomplex manner eminently, though not formally, includest all the infinite variety of complex ideas that are found among the creatures.' Such language as this may be indulged perhaps in secret by a man accustomed to thinking and meditating in these forms; but his fellow Christians would no more be edified by them than by his praying in an unknown tongue.

By the language of mystical divinity, I mean such incomprehensible sorts of phrases as a sect of divines among the papists have used, and some few Protestants too nearly imitated, such as 'the deiform fund of the soul', the 'superessential life', of 'singing a hymn of silence'; that God is 'an abyss of light', a 'circle whose centre is everywhere, and his circumference nowhere'; that hell is 'the dark world made up of spiritual sulphur and other ingredients not united or harmonised, and without that pure balsamical oil that flows from the heart of God'. These are great swelling words of vanity that captivate silly people into raptures by the mere sound without sense.

By running long metaphors, I mean the pursuing of a similitude or metaphor, and straining so far as to injure the doctrines of religion by a false sense or very improper expressions. Such was the language of a foolish writer, who bids us 'give our hearts to the Lord, cut them with the knife of contrition, take out the blood of your sins by confession, afterward wash it with satisfaction', etc.

By expressions that savour too much of party-zeal, I mean those that would be useless, if not offensive, to Christians of different persuasions that join with us in prayer. We should not in our prayers too much insist on the corruptions of doctrine and worship in any church, when some of that communion join with us; nor, for example, of infants' interest in the covenant of grace, and baptism the first seal of it, when Baptists are worshipping with us. Our prayers should not savour of anger and uncharitableness, for we are bid to lift up holy hands without wrath (*1 Tim.* 2:8).

When I recommend such expressions as are easy to be understood, it is evident that you should avoid long and entangled sentences, and place your thoughts and words in such an order that the heart of the hearers may be able to receive and join in the worship as fast as their ears receive the words. As in all our conversations, conferences and discourses, we should labour to make everything we say to be understood immediately, so especially in prayer, where the affections should be stirred. This cannot well be done if the hearers must take much pains to understand the meaning of what is said.

RULE 3: *Let your language be grave and decent, which is a medium between magnificence and lowliness.*

Let it be plain, but not coarse. Let it be clean, but not at all lofty and glittering. Job speaks of choosing his words to reason with God (*Job* 9:14). Some words are choice and beautiful; others are unseemly and disagreeable. Be careful of all wild, irregular and vain expressions that are unsuited to so solemn a part of worship. The best direction I can give you in this case is to use such language as you generally use in your serious discourses upon religious subjects, when you confer with one another about the things of God. For then the mind is disposed to gravity, and the tongue should answer and interpret the mind. The language of a Christian in prayer is the clothing of his thoughts or the dress of the soul, and it should be composed like the dress of his body: decent and neat, but not pompous or gaudy; simple and plain, but not careless, unclean or rude.

Avoid therefore glittering language and affected style. When you address God in worship, it is a fault to be ever borrowing phrases from the theatre and profane poets. This does not seem to be the language of Canaan. Many of their expressions are too light and wild and airy for so awesome a duty. An excessive fondness of elegance and fine style in prayer reveals the same pride and vanity of mind as an affectation of many jewels and fine apparel in the house of God. It betrays us into a neglect of our hearts and of experimental religion by an affectation to make the nicest speech and say the finest things we can, instead of sincere devotion and praying in the Spirit. Moreover, if we wish to deal in lofty phrases, Scripture itself sufficiently abounds with them; and these are the most agreeable to God and most affecting to his own people.

Avoid low and coarse and too-familiar expressions that may conjure any contemptible or ridiculous ideas, or raise any improper or irreverent thoughts, or base and impure images, in the mind; for these much injure the devotion of our fellow worshippers. It is a very culpable negligence to speak to God in such a rude and unseemly manner as would ill become us in the presence of our fellow creatures when we address ourselves to them. Not but that God hears the language of the meanest soul in secret, though he is not capable of expressing himself with all the decencies that are to be desired. Yet it is certain that we ought to seek to equip ourselves with becoming methods of expression, so that our performance of this duty may be pleasing to those with whom we worship.

We need not be rough and slovenly in order to be sincere. Sometimes persons have been guilty of great improprieties and exposed religion to profane scoffing by a too familiar mention of the name of Christ and by irreverent freedoms when they speak to God. I cannot approve of the phrases of 'rolling upon Christ', of 'swimming upon Christ to dry land', of 'taking a lease of Christ for all eternity'. I think we may fulfil the command of coming boldly to the throne of grace without such language. Persons are sometimes in danger of improprieties in borrowing low and trivial, or unseemly, similitudes. They search all the sinks of nastiness to fetch metaphors for their sins; and praying for the coming of Christ, they 'fold up the heavens like an old cloak', and 'shovel days out of the way'. By these few instances you may learn what to avoid. And remember that words, as well as things, grow old and displeasing. Some expressions, that might have appeared proper sixty years ago would be highly improper and offensive to the ears of the present age. It is therefore no sufficient apology for these phrases, that men of great learning and most eminent piety have made use of them.

> RULE 4: *Seek after those ways of expression that denote the fervency of affection and carry life and spirit with them; that may awaken and exercise our love, our hope, our holy joy, our sorrow, our fear, and our faith, as well as express the activity of those graces.*

This is the way to raise, assist and maintain devotion. We should avoid the sort of style that looks more like preaching, which some persons that affect long prayers have been guilty of to a great degree. They have been speaking to the people, and teaching them the doctrines of religion and the mind and will of God, rather than speaking to God the desires of their own minds. They have wandered away from God to preach to men. But this is quite contrary to the nature of prayer; for prayer is our own address to God, declaring our sense of divine things and pouring out our hearts before him with warm and proper affections.

There are several modes of expression that promote this end:

i. *Exclamations*, which serve to set forth an affectionate wonder, a sudden surprise, or violent impression of anything on the mind. 'O how great is thy goodness, which thou hast laid up for them that fear thee!' (*Psa.* 31:19).

'How precious are thy thoughts unto me, O God! how great is the sum of them!' (*Psa.* 139:17). 'O wretched man that I am! who shall deliver me?' (*Rom.* 7:24).

ii. *Interrogations*, when the plain sense of anything we declare to God is turned into a question to make it more emphatic. 'Whither shall I go from thy Spirit? or whither shall I flee from thy presence?' (*Psa.* 139:7). 'Do I not hate them, O Lord, that hate thee?' (*Psa.* 139:21). 'Who shall deliver me from the body of this death? (*Rom.* 7:24).

iii. *Appeals to God*, concerning our own needs or sorrows, our sincere and deep sense of the things we speak to him. 'Lord thou knowest all things; thou knowest that I love thee' (*John* 21:17). So David appeals to God, 'My sins are not hid from thee' (*Psa.* 69:5). 'Thou tellest my wanderings; are not my tears in thy book?' (*Psa.* 56:8). 'Thou knowest that I am not wicked. My witness is in heaven, and my record is on high' (*Job* 10:7; 16:19).

iv. *Expostulations,* which are indeed one particular sort of interrogation and are fit not only to express deep dejections of the mind, but to enforce any argument that is used in pleading with God, either for mercy for his saints or for the destruction of his enemies. 'Look down from heaven, and behold from the habitation of thy holiness and of thy glory: where is thy zeal and thy strength, the sounding of thy bowels and thy mercies toward me? are they restrained? O Lord, why hast thou made us to err from thy ways, and hardened our heart from thy fear?' (*Isa.* 63:15, 17). 'Awake, awake, put on strength, O arm of the Lord: Art thou not it that hath cut Rahab, and wounded the dragon? Art thou not it which hath dried the sea, the waters of the great deep?' (*Isa.* 51:9, 10). 'Will the Lord cast off for ever? and will he be favourable no more?' (*Psa.* 77:7). 'O Lord God of hosts, how long wilt thou be angry?' (*Psa.* 80:4). 'Wherefore hidest thou thy face, and forgettest our affliction?' (*Psa.* 44:24). God invites his people thus to argue with him, 'Come now let us reason together, saith the Lord' (*Isa.* 1:18). And holy men in humble and reverent expostulations have with many reasons pleaded their cause before God, and their words are recorded as our patterns.

v. *Options,* or wishes, fit to set forth serious and earnest desires, 'Oh that I might have my request' (*Job* 6:8). 'O that my ways were directed to keep thy statutes!' (*Psa.* 119:5).

vi. *Apostrophes;* that is, when in the midst of our addresses to God we abruptly turn away from the speech, and turn to our own souls, being led by the vehemence of some sudden devout thought. So David (*Psa.* 16:1–2): 'Preserve me, O God: for in thee do I put my trust. O my soul, thou hast said unto the Lord, Thou art my Lord.' In meditations, psalms, hymns or other devotional compositions, these apostrophes may be longer and more frequent, but in prayer they should be very short, except when the speech is turned from one person of the blessed Trinity to another, as: 'Great God, hast thou not promised that thy Son should have the heathen for his inheritance, and that he should rule the nations? Blessed Jesus, how long before thou assume this kingdom? When wilt thou send thy Spirit to enlighten and convert the world? When, O eternal Spirit, wilt thou come and shed abroad thy light and thy grace, through all the earth?'

vii. *Ingeminations,* or redoubling our expressions, which argue an eager and inflamed affection. 'O Lord God to whom vengeance belongeth; O God, to whom vengeance belongeth, shew thyself' (*Psa.* 94:1, 2). 'My soul waiteth for the Lord more than they that watch for the morning: I say, more than they that watch for the morning' (*Psa.* 130:6). And the conclusion of Psalm 72 is, 'Blessed be his glorious name for ever; Amen, and Amen'.

But here let us take care to distinguish between those repetitions that arise from real fervency of spirit, and those that are used merely to lengthen out a prayer or that arise from mere barrenness of heart and lack of content. It is far better, at least in public prayer, to yield to our present indisposition and shorten the duty, than to fill up our time with constant repetitions, such as, 'O Lord our God, if it be thy blessed will; we entreat thee; we beseech thee; O Lord, have mercy upon us.' For though some of these expressions may be properly enough repeated several times in a prayer, filling up every empty space and stretching out almost every sentence with them is not agreeable to our fellow worshippers, nor a help to our devotion or theirs.

> RULE 5: *Do not always confine yourselves to one set form of words to express any particular request, nor take too much pains to avoid an expression merely because you used it in prayer before.*

Do not be overfond either of an exact uniformity of words or of perpetual diversity of expression in every prayer. It is best to keep the middle between these two extremes. We should seek indeed to be equipped with a rich variety of holy language, that our prayers may always have something new and something engaging in them, and not tie ourselves to express one thing always in one set of words, lest this make us grow formal and dull and indifferent in those petitions. But on the other hand, if we are guilty of perpetually using new words which we never before used, we shall sometimes miss our own best and most spiritual meaning, and many times be driven to great impropriety of speech. Our prayers by this means will look like the fruit of our fancy, and invention, and labour of the head, more than the breathings of the heart. The imitation of those Christians and ministers that have the best gifts will be an excellent direction in this case, as well as in the former cases.

The Voice in Prayer

THE BEAUTY OF OUR EXPRESSIONS and the tunefulness of our voice can never render our worship more acceptable to God, the infinite Spirit; yet our natures, being composed of flesh and spirit, may be assisted in worship by the harmony of the voice of the speaker. The content, method and expressions may be ever so well chosen in prayer, but it is possible for the voice to spoil the pleasure and injure the devotion of our fellow worshippers. When speeches of the best composition and the warmest language are recited in a cold, harsh or ungrateful way, the beauty of them is almost lost.

Some persons, by nature, have a very sweet and tuneful voice, and whatever they speak appears pleasing. Others must take many more pains and follow rules and directions diligently, that their voice may be formed to an agreeable pronunciation. For we find by sad experience that all the advantages that nature can supply to assist our devotions are too little to keep our hearts from wandering and to maintain delight. At least it is necessary to recognise and avoid those disagreeable ways of pronunciation that may disgust those who join with us rather than edify.

In secret prayer there is no necessity of a voice, for God hears a whisper as well as a sigh and a groan. Yet some

Christians cannot pray with any advantage to themselves without the use of their voice in some degree. Nor can I judge it at all improper, but rather, preferable, that you have a convenient place for secrecy. For you will not only stir up your own affections the more; but by practice in secret, if you take due care of your voice there, you may learn also to speak the better in public.

The great and general rule I would lay down for managing the voice in prayer is this: let us use the same voice with which we usually speak in grave and serious conversation, especially upon intense and affecting subjects. This is the best direction that I know to regulate the sound as well as the words. Our own native and common voice appears most natural and may be managed with greatest ease. And some persons have taken occasion to ridicule our worship and to censure us as hypocrites, when we fondly seek and affect any new and different sort of sounds or voices in our prayers.

The particular directions are such as these:

DIRECTION 1: *Let your words all be pronounced distinctly and not made shorter by cutting off the last syllable, nor longer, by adding 'hem' or 'o', long breaths, affected groanings and useless sounds, coughing, etc., which some have been guilty of and have sufficiently disgraced religion.*

If you cut off and lose the last syllable of your word, or mumble the last words of the sentence and sink in your voice so that others cannot hear, they will be ready to think it is because you did not speak properly and so were afraid to be heard.

If, on the other hand, you lengthen out your sentences with ridiculous sounds, you endanger the devotion of even the wisest and best of your fellow worshippers and expose the worship to profane jest. While you seem to be clearing your throat or expressing greater affection by such methods, others will suspect that it is a method only to prolong your sentences, to stretch your prayers and to recover your thoughts of what to say next. Therefore when your passions happen to be elevated with some lively expression in prayer and you are delightfully constrained to dwell upon it, or when you meditate to speak the next sentence with propriety, it is far better to make a long pause and keep a decent silence than to fall into making extraneous sounds.

DIRECTION 2: *Let every sentence be spoken loudly enough to be heard, yet not so loud as to affright or offend the ear.*

Between these two extremes there is a great variety of degrees in sound, sufficient to satisfy all the changes of our emotions and the different sense of every part of our prayer. In the beginning of prayer especially, a lower voice is more becoming, as it signifies both humility and reverence when we enter into the presence of God. It is also a great convenience to the organs of speech not to arise too high at first, for it is much harder to sink again afterwards than to rise to higher accents, if it is required. Some persons have a habit of beginning their prayers, even upon the most common family occasions, so loudly as to startle the company; others begin so low in a large assembly that it looks like secret worship and as though they forbid those present to join with them. Both these extremes are to be avoided by prudence and moderation.

DIRECTION 3: *Observe a due medium between excessive swiftness and slowness of speech, for both are faulty in their way.*

If you are too swift, your words will be hurried; they will run on to one another and be mingled in confusion. It is necessary to observe a due distance between your words, and a much greater distance between your sentences, that so all may be pronounced distinctly and intelligibly.

Due and proper pauses and stops will give the hearer time to conceive and reflect on what you speak and to join with you more heartily; and it will allow you to breathe and make the work easier and more pleasant for yourselves. Moreover, when persons run on heedlessly with an incessant flow of words, being carried, as it were, in a violent stream, without rests or pauses, they are in danger of uttering things rashly before God, giving no time at all to their own meditation, but indulging their tongue to run sometimes too fast for their own thoughts as well as for the thoughts of those present with them. Some persons have begun a sentence in prayer and been forced to break off and begin a new: Or if they have pursued that sentence, it has been with so much inconsistency that it could hardly be reduced to sense or grammar. This has given too obvious an occasion to others to ridicule all conceived prayer and has been very dishonourable to God and his worship. And all this arises from a hurry of the tongue into the middle of a sentence before the mind has conceived the full and complete sense of it.

On the other hand, if you are too slow, and very perceptibly and remarkably so, this will grow tiresome to the hearers. They will have taken in the sentence you spoke last, and wait in pain, and long for the next expression to stimulate their thoughts and carry on their devotion. This will make our worship appear heavy and dull. Yet I must say that an error in prayer of this sort is to be preferred to an excess of speed and hurry, and its consequences are less hurtful to religion.

In general, with regard to the two foregoing directions, let the sense of each sentence be a rule to guide your voice, whether it must be high or low, swift or leisurely. In the invocation of God, in humble adoration, in confession of sin, and self-resignation, a slower and a more modest voice is for the most part very becoming, as well as in every other part of prayer where there is nothing very emotional expressed. But in petitions, in pleadings, in thanksgiving and rejoicing in God, fervency and importunity, holy joy and triumph will raise the voice some degrees higher, and lively passions of the delightful kind will naturally draw out our language with greater speed and spirit.

DIRECTION 4: *Let proper expression be used, according to what the sense requires.*

It would be endless to give particular rules on proper expression. Nature dictates this to everyone, if we will but heed the dictates of nature. Yet in order to attain it in greater perfection and to secure us from irregularity in this point, let us avoid the following few things:

i. Avoid a constant uniformity of voice, that is, when every word and sentence are spoken without any difference in sound, like a boy at school repeating all his lesson in one dull note, which shows that he is not truly acquainted with the sense and value of the author. Now though persons who speak without any difference of accent may be truly sincere and devout, such pronunciation will appear to others as careless and negligent, as though the person that speaks were unconcerned about the great work in which he is engaged and as though he had none of his feelings moved to modulate his voice into agreeable changes.

ii. Avoid a faulty placement of the accents and false pronunciation. One kind of faulty pronunciation is when a person uses just the same set of accents and repeats the same set of sounds and cadences in every sentence, though his sentences are ever so different in their sense, length, or warmth of expression; for example, if a man should begin every sentence in prayer with a high voice and end it in a low; or begin each line with a hoarse and deep bass and end it with a shrill and sharp sound. This is as if a musician should have but one sort of tune or one single set of notes and repeat it over again in every line of a song, which could never be graceful.

Another instance of false pronunciation is when strong accents are put upon little words and particles which bear no great force in the sentence. Some persons are so inept that the little words 'they' and 'that' and 'of' and 'by' have the biggest force of the voice bestowed upon them, whilst the phrases and expressions of chief significance are spoken with a cold and low voice.

Another example of false pronunciation is when a calm plain sentence, in which there is nothing fervent, is delivered with much force and violence of speech; or when the most fervent and emotional expressions are spoken with the utmost calmness and composure of voice. All of these are very unnatural in themselves and to be avoided by those who wish to speak properly, to the edification of those who worship with them.

The last instance I shall mention of false pronunciation is when we fall into a musical turn of voice, as though we were singing instead of praying. Some devout souls have been betrayed into such a self-pleasing tone by the warmth of their spirits in secret worship, and having no one to hear and inform them how disagreeable it is to others, have indulged it even to an incurable habit.

iii. Avoid excessively colouring every word and sentence to extremes, as if you were upon a stage in a theatre. This fault also some serious persons have fallen into for lack of caution. And it has appeared so like affectation that it has given great ground for censure.

One example is to express every humble and mournful sentence in a weeping tone and impersonate someone that is actually crying. That is what our adversaries have exposed by the name of canting and whining, and have thrown blame upon a whole party because of the imprudence of a few.

Another instance of this excessive affectation is when we express every pleasurable sentence in our prayers, every promise or comfort, every joy or hope, in too free and airy a manner, with too bold an exultation, or with a broad smile. These indeed look like too familiar a dealing with the great God. Every odd and unpleasant tone should be banished from divine worship. Nor should we appear before God in humility upon our knees yet with grandeur and magnificence upon our tongues, lest the sound of our voice should contradict our gesture, lest it should savour of irreverence in so awful a pretence and give disgust to those that hear us.

Gesture in Prayer

IT MAY NOT so properly be termed a part of the gift; yet inasmuch as it belongs to the outward performance of this piece of worship, I cannot think it improper to mention gesture here.

Since we are commanded to pray always and at all times, there can be no posture of the body unfit for short ejaculations and pious breathings towards God: while we lie in our beds, while we sit at our tables, or while we are taking our rest in any methods of refreshment, our souls may go out towards our heavenly Father and have sweet converse with him in short prayers. And to this we must refer that passage concerning David, where it is said: 'David sat before the Lord, and said, Who am I, O Lord God, and what is mine house, that thou hast brought me hitherto?' (*1 Chron.* 17:16). But when we draw near to God in special times of worship, the work of prayer calls for a greater solemnity; and in everything that relates to it we ought to compose ourselves with greater reverence, that we may worship God with our bodies as well as with our spirits, and pay him devotion with our whole natures (*1 Cor.* 6:20).

In our discourse concerning gestures fit for worship, we shall consider firstly the posture of the whole body, and secondly, of the particular parts of it; and we will endeavour to secure you against improprieties in either of them.

i. Those postures of the body which the light of nature and rule of Scripture seem to dictate as most proper for prayer are standing, kneeling or prostration.

Prostration is sometimes used in secret prayer, when a person is under a deep and uncommon sense of sin and falls flat upon his face before God and pours out his soul before him, under the influence of such thoughts and the working of such graces as produce very uncommon expressions of humiliation and self-abasement. This we find made use of in Scripture upon many occasions: Abraham fell on his face before God (*Gen.* 17:3), and

Joshua before the Lord Jesus Christ, the captain of the host of God (*Josh.* 5:14). So Moses, Ezekiel and Daniel at other times; so in the New Testament, when John fell at the feet of the angel to worship him, supposing it to have been our Lord (*Rev.* 19:10). And who could not but fall down to the dust at the presence of God himself?

Kneeling is the most frequent posture used in this worship, and nature seems to dictate and lead us to it as an expression of humility, of a sense of our needs, of supplication for mercy, and of adoration of, and dependence upon, him before whom we kneel. This posture has been practised in all ages and in all nations, even where the light of Scripture has never shined. And if it might be done conveniently, it would certainly be a most agreeable posture for the worship of God in public assemblies, as well as in private families or in our secret chambers. There are so many instances and directions for this posture in Scripture that it would be useless to take pains to prove it: we mention Solomon (*2 Chron.* 6:13); Ezra (*Ezra* 9:5); Daniel (*Dan.* 6:10); Christ himself (*Luke* 22:41); Paul (*Acts* 20:36; 21:5 and *Eph.* 3:14).

Lastly, standing is a posture not unfit for this worship, especially in places where the humbler gestures are not convenient. For as standing up before a person whom we respect and reverence is a token of that esteem and honour which we pay him, so standing before God, where we have not conveniences of kneeling, is an agreeable testimony to our high esteem of him whom we then address and worship. There are instances of this gesture in the Word of God. Our Saviour says to his disciples, 'When ye stand praying' (*Mark* 11:25); and the publican stood afar off and prayed (*Luke* 18:13). Standing seems to have been the common gesture of worship in a large public assembly (*2 Chron.* 20:4–5, 13). And in this case it is very proper to conform to the custom of Christians with whom we worship, whether standing or kneeling, since neither of them are made absolutely necessary by the Word of God.

But I cannot think that sitting, or other postures of rest and laziness, ought to be indulged in solemn times of prayer, unless persons are in some respect infirm or aged, or the work of prayer is so long as to make it troublesome to maintain the one posture. In these cases, whatever gesture of body keeps the mind in the best composure and fits it most to proceed in this worship, not only will be accepted of God, but is most agreeable to him. For it is a great rule that he has given, and he will always stand by, that bodily exercise profits little; for he looks chiefly on the heart, and he will have mercy and not sacrifice.

ii. The posture of the several parts of the body that are most agreeable to worship and that may protect us from all improprieties, may be particularized and enumerated:

As for the head, let it be kept for the most part without motion, for there are very few turns of the head in this part of worship that can be accounted proper. And many persons have exposed themselves to ridicule by tossing and shaking the head and nodding while they have been offering the solemn sacrifice of prayer to God. Yet it must be allowed that in cases of great humiliation, the hanging down of the head is no improper method to express that temper of mind. So the praying publican in the text cited above; so the Jews in the time of Ezra, who in a full congregation bowed their heads and worshipped the Lord with their faces toward the ground (*Neh.* 8:6). But in our expressions of hope and joy, it is natural to lift up the head while we believe that our redemption draws nigh (*Luke* 21:28). I might also mention the apostle's advice, that he that prays ought to have his head uncovered, lest he dishonour his head (*1 Cor.* 11:4).

The God of nature has written in the face various indications of the temper of the mind, and especially when it is moved by any warm emotion.

In divine worship the whole visage should be composed to gravity and solemnity, to express a holy awe and reverence of the majesty of God and the high importance of the work in which we are engaged.

In confession of sin, while we express the sorrows of our souls, melancholy will appear in our countenances. The dejection of the mind may be read there and, according to the language of Scripture, shame and confusion will cover our faces. The humble sinner blushes before God at the remembrance of his guilt (*Jer.* 51:51; *Ezra* 9:6). Fervency of spirit in our petitions, and holy joy when we give thanks to our God for his mercies, and rejoice in our highest hope, will be revealed by very agreeable and pleasing traces in the features and countenance.

But here let us take heed that we do not expose ourselves to the censure of our Saviour, who reproved the Pharisees for disfiguring their faces all that day which they set apart for secret fasting and prayer (*Matt.* 6:16). While we are engaged in the very duty, some decent appearances of the devotion of the mind in the countenance are very natural and proper, and are not here forbidden by our Lord. But at the same time, it is best that those indications or characters of the countenance should fall below and stay behind the inward affections of the mind, rather than rise too high or go before. The devotion of our hearts should be warmer and stronger than that of our faces. And we should beware of all irregular and disagreeable distortions of the face, all those affected grimaces and wringing of the countenance, as it were, to squeeze out our words or our tears, which sometimes may tempt our fellow worshippers to disgust when they see us. We must also, on the other hand, avoid yawning and an air of lifelessness and drowsy gestures, which reveal the sloth of the mind. It is a terrible word spoken by Jeremiah in another case, 'Cursed be he that doeth the work of the Lord negligently' (*Jer.* 48:10).

To lift up the eyes to heaven is a very natural posture of prayer, and therefore the psalmist so often mentions it (*Psa.* 121:1; 123:1; 141:8). Though sometimes under great dejection of spirit and concern for sin, it is very decent with the publican to look down as it were upon the ground, as being unworthy to lift up our eyes to heaven where God dwells (*Luke* 18:13).

But above all, a roving eye that takes notice of every-thing ought to be avoided in prayer. For though it may be possible for a person that prays to keep his thoughts composed whilst his eyes wander (which at the same time seems very difficult), spectators will be ready to judge that our hearts are given to wander as much as our eyes are, and they will suspect that the life and spirit of devotion is absent. Upon this account some persons have found it most agreeable to keep the eyes always closed in prayer, lest by the objects that occur to their sight, the chain of their thoughts should be broken or their hearts led away from God by their senses. Nor can I think it improper to shut that door of the senses and exclude the world while we are conversing with God. But in this and other directions, I would always excuse those persons with any natural weaknesses, and they must use those methods that make the work of prayer easiest for them.

The lifting up of the hands, sometimes folded together, or sometimes apart, is a very natural expression of our seeking help from God, who dwells above (*Psa.* 28:2; 134:2). The elevation of the eyes and the hands is so much the dictate of nature in all acts of worship in which we address God that even the heathens have frequently practised it, as we can see in the accounts of their many writers. We also find it mentioned as the practice of the saints in the Holy Scripture.

And as the elevation of the hands to heaven is a very natural gesture when a person prays for himself, so when a superior prays for a blessing to descend upon a person of an inferior character, it is very natural to lay his hand upon the head of the person for whom he prays. This we find practised from the beginning of the world, and the practice descends throughout all ages. It is true indeed that this gesture, the imposition of hands, was used by the prophets and apostles when they pronounced authoritative and divine blessings upon men and communicated miraculous gifts. But I esteem it not so much a peculiar rite belonging to the prophetic benediction, as it is a natural expression of a desire of the divine blessing from a father to a son, from an elder person to a younger, from a minister to other Christians, especially those who are babes in Christ. Therefore when a person is set apart and devoted to God in any solemn office, whilst prayers are made for a divine blessing to descend upon him, imposition of hands seems to be a gesture of nature and, considered in itself, I cannot think it either unlawful or necessary.

With regard to other parts of the body, there is little need of any directions. Calmness and quietness and a uniformity of posture seem to be more decent. Almost all motions are disagreeable, especially those that carry with them any sound or noise, for then the worship is disturbed rather than promoted, and some persons by such actions have seemed as though they beat time to the music of their own sentences.

In secret devotion indeed, where we give vent to our warmest passions, sighs, groans and weeping may be very well allowed, and our whole nature and frame is moved with devout affections of the mind. But in public these things should be less indulged, except in such extraordinary times that all the assembly may be effectually convinced that they arise deep from the heart. If we indulge ourselves in various motions or noise made by the hands or feet or any other parts, it will tempt others to think that our minds are not very intensely engaged, or it will appear that we display a familiarity and irreverence that we would not willingly be guilty of in the presence of our superiors here on earth.

Family prayer

Since it is so necessary for the person that speaks in prayer to abstain from noisy motions, I hope that all who join with him will understand that it is very unseemly for them to disturb the worship with motion and noise. How improper it is at family prayer for persons to spend a good part of the time in settling themselves upon their knees, adjusting their dress, moving their chairs, saluting those that pass by and come in after the worship is begun. How unbecoming it is to stir and rise while the two or three last sentences are spoken, as though devotion were so unpleasant and tedious a thing that they longed to have it over. How often it is found that the knee is the only part that pays external reverence to God, while all the other parts of the body are disposed to laziness, ease and negligence. There are some that seldom come in till the prayer is begun, and then a bustle and disturbance is made for their accommodation. To prevent some of these irregularities, I would persuade him that prays not to begin till all that intend to join in the family worship are present, and that even before the chapter is read; for I would not have the Word of God used in a family for no other purpose than the tolling of a bell at church, to tell that the people are coming in to prayers.

Grace before and after meals

Since I have spoken so particularly about family prayer, I would insert a word or two concerning another part of social worship in a family, and that is giving thanks before and after meals. We ought to have a due regard to that occasion and the persons present; its neglect has been attended with improprieties and indiscretions.

Some have accustomed themselves to muttering a few words with a very low voice, as though by some secret charm they were to consecrate the food alone and there was no need of the rest to join with them in the petitions. Others have broken out into so violent a sound that they seemed bound to make a thousand people hear them.

Some perform this part of worship with a light and familiar air, as though they had no sense of the great God to whom they speak; others have put on an unnatural solemnity and changed their natural voice into so different and awkward a tone, not without some distortions of countenance, that strangers have been tempted to ridicule.

It is the custom of some to hurry over a single sentence or two, and they are finished before half the company are prepared to lift up a thought to heaven. And some have been heard to speak a blessing on the church and the king, but seem to have forgotten that they were giving thanks for the food they have received and asking God to bless it. Others again have gone into a long prayer and, among a multitude of other petitions, have not had one that related to the table before them.

The general rules of prudence, together with a due observation of the custom of the place where we live, would correct all these disorders and teach us that a few sentences suited to the occasion, spoken with an audible and proper voice, are sufficient for this purpose, especially if any strangers are present. If we are out in mixed company, many times it is best for each person to lift up a petition to God in secret for himself. But in a religious family, or where all the company are in agreement and no other circumstance forbids it, I cannot disapprove of a pious soul sometimes breathing out a few devout expressions more than are just necessary to give thanks for the food we receive. Nor is it improper to include any other present occurrence of providence together with the table worship.

Here I would also wish to add this: that when a person is eating alone, I do not see any necessity of rising always from his seat to recommend his food to the blessing of God, which may be done in any posture of body with a short ejaculation. Yet in company, I am of the opinion that the present custom of standing up is more decent and honourable than of sitting down just before we give thanks, which was practised too often in a former age.

I have expressed my sentiments concerning the gestures proper for prayer. I hope they will appear useful and proper to maintain the dignity of the worship and to pay honour to God with our bodies as well as with our souls. As we must not make ourselves mere statues and lifeless engines of prayer, neither must we, out of pretence of spirituality, neglect all proprieties. Our forms of religion are not as numerous or ornate as the Jewish rites; nor are they theatrical gestures or superstitious fopperies like those of the papists. We have no need to be masters of ceremonies in order to worship God aright, if we will but attend to the simplicity of manners which nature dictates and follow the precepts and examples that the gospel confirms.

REMARK: Though the gestures that belong to preaching are very different from those of prayer, most of the rules that are prescribed for the expression and the voice in prayer may be usefully applied also to preaching. But the difference is that in the work of preaching the same restraints are not always necessary, especially in applying truth warmly to the conscience. For then we speak to men in the name and authority of God, and we may indulge a greater freedom and brightness of language, more lively motions and bolder efforts of zeal and outward fervour. But in prayer, where in the name of sinful creatures we address the great and holy God, everything that belongs to us must be composed to an appearance of humility.

General Directions on the Gift of Prayer

I SHALL CONCLUDE this chapter with these five general directions:

DIRECTION 1: *Keep the middle way between an exact and laborious attendance to all the rules I have given and a careless neglect of them.*

Every rule seems to carry its own reason, so it is proper that some regard should be given to it when occasions for the practice occur. For I have endeavoured to say nothing on this subject except what might in some way or other be useful towards the attainment of an agreeable gift of prayer and the decent exercise of that gift. The multiplicity of our shortcomings, the unfaithfulness of our memories, the dullness and slowness of our apprehensions, the common wanderings of our thoughts, and the coldness of our affections, will require our best care for the remedy of them.

Yet, on the other hand, I would not have you confine yourselves too precisely to all these forms in content, method, expression, voice and gesture upon every occasion, lest you feel yourselves under some restraint and deprive your souls of that divine liberty with which upon special occasions the Spirit of God blesses his own people in the performance of this duty. When the heart is full of good matter, the tongue will sometimes be as the pen of a ready writer (*Psa.* 65:1). Such a fixedness and fullness of thought, such a fervour of pious affections, will sometimes produce so glorious a fluency and variety of pertinent and moving expressions that it appears the man is carried beyond himself and would be constrained and cramped by a careful adherence to rules.

See then that the graces of prayer are at work in your souls with power. Let this be your first and highest care; and by a good influence this will lead you to a natural and easy performance of this duty according to most of the particular rules I have given, even without an exact observance of them – as, for example, a man may sometimes in a very musical mood, without adhering to the rules of art, strike out some inimitable graces and flourishes and charm all that hear him.

DIRECTION 2: *Observe those among ministers and fellow Christians who have the most edifying gifts.*

In content, method, expression, voice and gesture, endeavour to imitate those who are more universally approved of and who stir and maintain the devotion of all their fellow worshippers. And at the same time, also take notice of all the irregularities and improprieties that any persons are guilty of in this worship, in order to avoid them when you pray.

DIRECTION 3: *Use all proper means to obtain a manly presence of mind and holy courage in religious performances.*

Though excess of bashfulness is a natural weakness, it may become very culpable if indulged. Many useful gifts have been buried in silence through a sinful bashfulness. Generally all persons, when they first begin to pray in public, feel something of this weakness for want of a due presence of mind, and it has had different effects. Some persons have lost that due calmness and temper which should govern their expressions, and have been driven on to the end of their prayer like a schoolboy hurrying his lesson over, or an alarm set running that could not stop till it was quite down. Others have hesitated at every sentence, and even felt a halt in their speech and could utter no more. Others again, whose minds were well equipped and prepared, have lost their own scheme of thoughts and made poor work at first, through mere bashfulness.

I grant that courage and a degree of assurance are natural talents, but it may also in a great measure be acquired by the use of proper means. I will mention a few of them.

i. Get above the shame of appearing religious, that you may be dead to the reproaches of a wicked world; and despise the jests and scandal that are cast upon strict godliness.

ii. Make religious conversation your practice and delight. If you are accustomed to speaking to men concerning the things of God without blushing, you will be enabled to speak to God in the presence of men with holy confidence.

iii. Strive to attain this gift of prayer to a tolerable degree, and exercise it often in secret for a considerable time before you begin in public.

iv. Take heed that your heart is always well prepared, and let the content of your prayer be well premeditated when you make your first public attempts.

v. Strive to maintain a much greater awe of the majesty of that God to whom you speak than of the opinions of the fellow creatures with whom you worship, that so you may, as it were, forget you are in the company of men while you address the most high God. Chide your heart into courage when you find it shy and sinking, and say, 'Dare I speak to the great and dreadful God, and shall I be afraid of man?'

In order to practise this advice well, the next is akin to it:

vi. Do not be too sensitive of your own reputation in these externals of religion. This softness of spirit which we call bashfulness often has a great deal of fondness for self mingled with it. When we are to speak in public, this enfeebles the mind, throws us into a hurry and makes us perform much worse than we do in secret. When we are satisfied that we are engaged in present duty to God, let us maintain a noble negligence of the censures of men and speak with the same courage as though none but God were present.

And to administer further relief under this weakness, I add:

vii. Make your first attempts in the company of one or two, either your inferiors or your most intimate, most pious and candid acquaintance, that you may be under no fear or concern about their opinions of your performance. Or join yourself with some young Christians of equal standing and set apart times for praying together; this is an excellent way to obtain the gift of prayer.

viii. Do not aim at length of prayer in your younger attempts, but rather be short. Offer up a few more common and necessary requests at first, and proceed by degrees to enlarge and fulfil the several parts of this worship, as further occasion offers and as your gifts and courage increase.

ix. Do not be discouraged if your first experiments are not as successful as you desire. Many a Christian has in time arrived at a glorious gift in prayer, who in their younger essays have been overwhelmed with bashfulness and confusion. Do not let Satan prevail with you by this temptation to cast off this practice and your hope at once.

x. Make it the matter of your earnest requests to God that you may be endowed with Christian courage, with a holy liberty of speech and with freedom of utterance, as the blessed Apostle Paul often prayed. You have reason to hope that he who gives every good and perfect gift will not deny you that which is so necessary to the performance of your duty.

DIRECTION 4: *Ask the assistance of a kind Christian friend to notice all the irregularities that you may be guilty of in prayers, especially in your first years of the practice of this duty.*

And consider those the most valuable of your friends, who will put themselves to the trouble of giving you a modest and an obliging hint of any of your own imperfections. For it is not possible for us to judge of the tone of our own voice or the gestures that we ourselves use, and whether they are agreeable to our fellow worshippers. And in other instances also, our friends may form a more unbiased judgement than ourselves and therefore are most fit to be our correctors.

For want of this, some persons in their youth have developed bad habits when speaking in public and exercising of the gift of prayer: ill tones, improper accents, wild facial distortions, and various other improprieties, which they carried with them all the years of their life. These have often exposed the worship of God to contempt and hindered rather than promoted the edification of those that join with them.

DIRECTION 5: *Be frequent in the practice of this duty of prayer, not only in secret, but with one another.*

For even if every rule that I have given, were fixed in your memories and always at hand, still without frequent practice you will never attain to any great skill and readiness in this holy exercise.

As our graces themselves, by being often tried and put to action, become stronger and shine brighter, give God more glory and do more service to men, so will it fare with every gift of the Holy Spirit also; it is developed by frequent exercise. Therefore the apostle tells the young evangelist Timothy not to neglect to stir up the gift that is in him, though the gift was communicated in an extraordinary way, by the imposition of hands (*2 Tim.* 1:6). And that is why some serious Christians who have less knowledge will exceed, in the gift of prayer, persons of great learning, wit, and judgement: because, though they do not understand the rules so well, they practise much more. And for the most part, if all other circumstances are equal, it will be found a general truth that he that prays most prays best.

CHAPTER 3

The Grace of Prayer

I n the first two chapters, I wrote concerning the external parts of prayer. I shall now briefly address the internal and spiritual part of that duty. This has been usually called *the grace of prayer.*

I shall endeavour to explain what it means and show how properly the term is used. Afterwards I shall particularly mention those inward and spiritual exercises of the mind which are required in the duty of prayer, and then give directions how to attain them.

But in most of this chapter I shall pass over things very briefly, because it is not my purpose to repeat what so many practical writers have said on these subjects.

The Grace of Prayer, and How It Differs from the Gift

GRACE, IN ITS MOST GENERAL SENSE, implies the free and undeserved favour of one person toward another that is esteemed his inferior. In the language of the New Testament, it is commonly used to signify the favour and mercy of God toward sinful creatures, which upon all accounts is acknowledged to be free and undeserved. Because our natures are corrupt and averse to what is good, whenever they are changed and inclined to

God and divine things, this is done by the power of God working in us. Therefore this very change of nature, this renewed and divine frame of mind, is called in the common language of Christians by the name of grace.

If I were to write my thoughts of the distinction between *virtue*, *holiness* and *grace*, I should give them thus:

Virtue generally signifies the mere material part of that which is good, without a particular reference to God as the principle or end. The dispositions and actions of the heathens were called virtues. And this word is also applied to sobriety, righteousness, charity, and everything that relates to ourselves and our neighbours, rather than to religion and things that relate to divine worship.

Holiness signifies all those good dispositions and actions having as their end particular reference to God, to whose glory they are devoted and performed. The word 'holy' signifies that which is devoted or dedicated.

Grace denotes the same dispositions, with a peculiar regard to God as their principle, intimating that they proceed from his favour.

Sometimes this word is used in a comprehensive sense to signify the whole train of Christian virtues or the universal habit of holiness. In this way we may understand these texts: 'Of his fullness we have received grace' (*John* 1:16); and 'Grow in grace, and in the knowledge of our Lord Jesus Christ' (*2 Pet.* 3:18). And so in our common language when we say that such a person is a graceless wretch, or he has no grace at all, we mean he has no good dispositions. And when we say someone is truly gracious, or has a principle of grace, we mean he is a man of religion and virtue.

Sometimes it is used in its singular sense, and means any one inclination or holy principle in the mind. So we say, the grace of faith, the grace of repentance, the grace of hope or love. 'Therefore, as ye abound in faith, in knowledge, and in your love to us, see that ye abound in this grace also [that is, generosity]' (*2 Cor.* 8:7).

Sometimes it is used in a broader, but not a universal, sense, and implies all those pious qualifications that belong to any one action or duty. So we read of the grace that belongs to conversation, 'Let your speech be always with grace' (*Col.* 4:6); the grace of singing: 'singing with grace in your hearts' (*Col.* 3:16); and the grace of divine worship seems to be mentioned: 'Let us have grace, whereby we may serve God acceptably, with reverence and godly fear' (*Heb.* 12:28). And the grace of prayer, ' I will pour on the house of David the Spirit of grace and of supplications' (*Zech.* 12:10).

In our common understanding, the grace of prayer is not any one single act or habit of the mind, but it implies all those holy dispositions of soul which are to be exercised in that part of divine worship. It consists in a readiness to put forth those acts of the sanctified mind, will and emotions which are suited to the duty of prayer.

And that is the great difference between the *gift* and the *grace* of prayer. The *gift* is but the outside, the shape of the duty. The *grace* is the soul and spirit that gives it life, vigour, and efficacy, that renders it acceptable to God and of real advantage to ourselves.

The *gift* chiefly consists in a readiness of thought appropriate to the various parts of prayer, and a facility of expressing those thoughts in speaking to God. The *grace* consists in the inward workings of the heart and conscience toward God and religion. The *gift* has a show and appearance of holy desires and affections; but holy affections, sincere desires, and real converse with God, belong only to the *grace* of prayer.

The gift and the grace are many times separated from each other, and it has been often found that the gift of prayer has been attained in a great degree by study and practice and by the common workings of the Spirit of God communicated to some persons who have known nothing of true grace. There may be also the grace of prayer in lively exercise in some souls who have but a very small degree of this gift and hardly know how to form their thoughts and desires into a regular method or to express those desires in tolerable language.

Concerning some persons it may be said, as in Matthew 7, that though they could pour out abundance of words before God in prayer, though they could preach like apostles or like angels, or cast out devils in the name of Christ, our Lord Jesus does not know them, for they have no grace. On the other hand, there are some who are dear to God and can but chatter and cry like a swallow or a crane, as Hezekiah did, and yet are in the lively exercise of the grace of prayer. But where both these, the gift and the grace, meet together in one person, such a Christian brings honour to God and has a greater capacity and prospect of doing much service for souls in the world. He is made of great use to the edification and comfort of his fellow Christians.

Those acts of the sanctified soul in all its powers which are put forth in the duty of prayer may be properly called so many graces of the Holy Spirit drawn forth into exercise. Of these, some belong to the whole work and worship of prayer, and others are specific to the various parts of the duty.

General Graces of Prayer

THE GRACES THAT belong to the whole work or duty of prayer, are such as these.

1. *Faith or belief in the being of God,* and his perfect knowledge, and his gracious notice of all that we speak in prayer. The apostle gives this rule: 'He that cometh to God must believe that he is, and that he is a rewarder of them that diligently seek him' (*Heb.* 11:6). We should endeavour to impress our minds frequently with a fresh and lively belief of God's existence, though he is so unknown; of his presence, though he is invisible; and of his just and merciful regard to all the actions of men, and especially their religious affairs. We do this so that prayer may not be a matter of custom and ceremony, but performed with the purpose and hope of pleasing God and getting some good from him. This exercise of a lively faith runs through every part of the duty and gives spirit and power to the whole worship.

2. *Gravity, solemnity and seriousness of spirit.* Let a light and trivial temper be utterly banished when we come into the presence of God. When we speak to the great Creator, who must also be our Judge, about the concerns of infinite and everlasting importance, we ought to have our souls clothed with solemnity and not to assume those airs which are lawful at other times, when we talk with our fellow creatures about ordinary affairs. Wantonness and vanity of mind ought never to be indulged in the least degree when we come to perform any part of divine worship, and especially when we, who are but dust and ashes, speak to the great and fearsome God.

3. *Spirituality and heavenly-mindedness* should run through the whole of this duty. For prayer is a retirement

from earth and a retreat from our fellow creatures to fix our attention on God and communicate with him who dwells in heaven. If our thoughts are full of corn and wine and oil, and the business of this life, we shall not seek so earnestly the favour and face of God, as becomes devout worshippers. The things of the world therefore must be commanded to stand by for a time and to abide at the foot of the mount, while we walk up higher to offer up our sacrifices, as Abraham did, and to meet our God.

Our aims, ends and desires should grow more spiritual as we proceed in this duty. And though God indulges us to converse with him about many of our temporal affairs in prayer, let us take care that the things of our souls and the eternal world always possess the chief room in our hearts. And whatever of the cares of this life enter into our prayers and are spread before the Lord, let us see that our aims are spiritual, that our very desires of earthly comforts may be purified from all carnal ends and sanctified to some divine purposes, to the glory of God, to the honour of the gospel and to the salvation of souls.

4. *Sincerity and uprightness of heart* is another grace that must run through this worship. Whether we speak to God concerning his own glories; whether we give him thanks for his abundant goodness or confess our various iniquities before him; or whether we express our desires of mercy at his hand; let our hearts and our lips agree, that we are not found mockers of God, who searches the heart and tries the reins, and can spy hypocrisy in the darkest corners of the soul.

5. *Holy watchfulness and intention of mind* upon the duty in which we are engaged must run through every part of prayer. Our thoughts must not be allowed to wander

among the creatures and rove to the ends of the earth when we come to converse with the high and holy God. Without this holy watchfulness we shall be in danger of leaving God in the midst of the worship, because the temptations that arise from Satan and from our own hearts are various and strong. Without this watchfulness our worship will degenerate into formality, and we shall find coldness and indifference creeping upon our spirits and spoiling the success of our duties. 'Watch unto prayer' is a constant direction of the great apostle.

To these I might add *humility and delight, or pleasure,* and other exercises of the sanctified affections. But I shall mention them more fully in the next section.

Graces that Belong to Particular Parts of Prayer

THE GRACES THAT belong particularly to the different parts of prayer are distinguished according to the parts of this duty:

1. *Invocation*, or calling upon God, requires a special awe of his majesty to accompany it, and a deep sense of our own lowliness and unworthiness. At the same time we should express holy wonder and pleasure that the most high God, who inhabits eternity, allows such contemptible and worthless beings as we to communicate with him.

2. *The work of adoration* or praise runs through the many attributes of the divine nature and requires of us the exercise of our various affections suited to those attributes. When we mention God's self-sufficiency and independence, it becomes us to be humble and acknowledge our dependence. When we speak of his power and of his wisdom, we should abase ourselves before him because of our weakness and folly, and stand in holy admiration at the infinity of those glories of God. When we mention

his love and compassion, our souls should return much love to him again, and our affections should go forth strongly towards him. When we think of his justice, we should have a holy awe upon our spirits and a religious fear suited to the presence of the just and dreadful God. And the thought of his forgiveness should awaken us to hope and joy.

3. In the *confession* of our sorrows and our sins, humility is a necessary grace, as well as deep contrition of soul, in the presence of that God whose laws we have broken, whose gospel we have abused, whose majesty we have affronted, and whose vengeance we have deserved. Here all the springs of repentance should be set open, and we should mourn for sin even at the same time that we hope iniquity is forgiven and our souls are reconciled to God. Shame, self-indignation and holy revenge against the corruption of our hearts should be awakened also in this part of prayer.

4. In our *petitions* we should raise our desires to such different degrees of fervency as the nature of our requests makes necessary. When we pray for the things of the upper world and eternal blessings, we cannot be too warm in our desires. When we seek the mercies of life, the degree of fervency should be abated, for it is possible that we may be happy and yet go without many of the comforts of the present state. Submission is here required. God expects to see his children thus rationally religious and wisely to divide the things that are most agreeable to his will and most necessary for our felicity.

While we make *intercession* for our friends or our enemies, we ought to feel in ourselves warm and lively compassion. And when we pray for the church of Christ in the world, we should animate all our expressions with a burning zeal for his glory and tenderness for our fellow Christians.

5. *Pleading* with God calls for humble importunity. For the arguments that we use with God in pleading with him are but the various forms of importunate request. But because we are but creatures, and we speak to God, humility ought to mingle with every one of our arguments. Our pleadings with him should be so expressed as always to carry in them that decency and that distance that becomes creatures in the presence of their Maker.

In pleading also we are required to exercise faith in the promises of the gospel, faith in the name of Christ Jesus our Mediator, and faith in the mercies of our God according to the revelations he has made of himself in his Word. We are called to believe that he is a rewarder of all who diligently seek him (*Heb*. 11:6); that he is a God who hears prayer and will bestow upon us what we seek, so far as is necessary for his glory and our salvation.

Here also the grace of hope comes into exercise. For while we trust the promises, we hope for the things promised or the things for which we petition. We ought to maintain an humble holy expectation of those mercies for which we plead with God. We must direct our prayer to him and look up with David (*Psa*. 5:3), and, with Habakkuk, 'stand upon our watch and see what he will say to us' (*Hab*. 2:1).

6. In the part of prayer called *profession*, or self-resignation, great humility is again required: a sweet submission to his will, a composed and quiet spirit under his determinations, even though, for reasons of infinite wisdom and love, he withholds from us the particular comforts that we seek. Here let patience be perfected, and let the soul continue in an humble frame, waiting upon

God. It should be with a divine steadiness of soul and the firmest courage of heart against all oppositions that we confirm all our self-dedications to the Lord.

7. In *thanksgiving*, a most hearty gratitude of soul is required: a deep sense of divine favours and a readiness to return to God according to his goodness, to the uttermost of our capacities; a growing love to God, and sincere longing to do something for him, correspondent to the variety and riches of his grace towards us. Here also, with holy wonder, we acknowledge the condescension of God to bestow mercies upon us who are so unworthy. And this wonder should arise and grow up into divine joy as we bless our Maker for the mercies of this life and our Father for an interest in his covenant and his special love. And in our thanksgiving, we should be sure to take notice of all responses to prayer, all merciful appearances of God in answer to our requests. For it is but a poor converse maintained with God if we care only about our speaking to him, but take no notice of any replies he condescends to make to our poor and worthless addresses.

8. When we *bless* God, we should show an earnest longing after the honour of the name of God, and our souls should breathe fervently after the accomplishment of those promises to spread his own honours, and to magnify his own name and the name of his Son. We should, as it were, exult and triumph in those glories which God, our God, possesses, and rejoice to think that he shall for ever possess them.

9. Then we conclude the whole prayer with our *Amen* of sincerity and of faith, in one short word expressing over again our adoration, our confessions and petitions, our trust and hope for the audience of our prayers and acceptance of our persons. From all these

we should take encouragement to rise from this duty with a sweet serenity and composure of mind, and maintain a joyful and heavenly frame as those who have been with God.

But lest some pious and humble souls be discouraged when they do not find these lively exercises of faith, hope, love, fervency of desire, and divine delight in worship, and from that conclude that they do not have the grace of prayer, I would add this caution: all the graces of prayer are seldom at work in the soul at once in a great and perceptible degree. Sometimes one prevails more, and sometimes another, in this feeble and imperfect state.

And when a Christian comes before God with much deadness of heart, much overcome with carnal thoughts, and feels great reluctance even to pray, and falls down before God, mourning, complaining, self-condemning, and with sighs and deep groans in secret makes known his burden and his sins to God; though he can speak but few words before him, such a frame and temper of mind will be approved of by that God who judges the secrets of the heart and makes most compassionate allowances for the infirmity of our flesh. He will acknowledge his own grace working in that soul, though it be just breathing and struggling upward through loads of sin and sorrow.

Directions to Attain the Grace of Prayer

IN ORDER TO direct us in the spiritual performance of this duty, we must consider it as a holy converse maintained between earth and heaven, between the great and holy God and mean and sinful creatures. Now the most natural rules that I can think of, to carry on this converse, are such as these:

DIRECTION 1: *Possess your hearts with a most affecting sense of the characters of the two parties that are to maintain this communication; that is, God and yourselves.*

This indeed is one direction for the gift of prayer, but it is also most necessary to attain the grace. Let us consider who this glorious being is who invites us to this fellowship with himself; how awesome in majesty! how fearsome in righteousness! how irresistible in power! how unsearchable in wisdom! how all-sufficient in blessedness! how condescending in mercy! Let us again consider who are we, that are invited to this communication: how vile in our original! how guilty in our hearts and lives! how needy of every blessing! how utterly incapable to help ourselves! and how miserable forever if we are without God!

And if we have sincerely obeyed the call of his gospel and have attained some comforting hope of his love, let us consider how infinite are our obligations to him, and how necessary; and how delightful it is to enjoy the visits here of the One with whom it will be our happiness to dwell forever. When we feel our spirits deeply impressed with such thoughts as these, we are in the best frame and most likely to pray with grace in our hearts.

DIRECTION 2: *When you come before God, remember the nature of this conversation.*

It is all spiritual; remember the dignity and privilege, the purpose and the importance of it. A sense of the high favour in being admitted to this privilege and honour will fill your souls with humble wonder and with heavenly joy, such as becomes the favourites and worshippers of an infinite God. A due attention to the purpose and importance of this duty will fix your thoughts to the most immovable attention and strict watchfulness; it will overspread your spirit with seriousness; it will command all your inward powers to devotion; and it will raise your desires to holy fervency. You pray to him who has power over your eternal salvation or eternal destruction, to save and to destroy. If eternity, with all its awesome import, will not awaken some of the graces of prayer, the soul must be in a very dull and insensible frame.

DIRECTION 3: *Seek earnestly a state of friendship with him with whom you converse, and labour after a good hope and assurance of that friendship.*

We are all by nature enemies of God and children of his wrath (*Rom.* 8:7; *Eph.* 2:2). If we are not reconciled, we can never hold communion with him. How can we delight to converse with an enemy so almighty or pay him due worship, while we believe he hates and will destroy us? But oh! how unspeakable is the pleasure in holding conversation with so infinite, so almighty, and so compassionate a friend! And how ready will all the powers of nature be to render every honour to him, while we feel and know ourselves to be his favourites and the children of his grace; while we believe that all his honours are our glory in this state of friendship, and each of his perfections are the pillars of our hope and the assurances of our happiness!

Now, in order to obtain this friendship and to promote this divine fellowship, I recommend you to the next direction:

DIRECTION 4: *Live much upon and with Jesus the Mediator, by whose interest alone you can come near God and be brought into his company.*

Christ is the way, the truth and the life; no one comes to the Father but by him (*John* 14:6). Through him Jews and Gentiles have access to the Father (*Eph.* 2:18). Live much upon him by trust and dependence, and live much with him by meditation and love.

When a sinner under first conviction sees with horror the dreadful holiness of God and his own guilt and desert of damnation, how fearful is he to draw near to God in prayer, and how discouraged while he abides without hope! But when he first beholds Christ in his mediatorial offices and his glorious all-sufficiency to save; when he first beholds this new and living way of access to God, consecrated by the blood of Christ, how cheerfully does he come before the throne of God and pour out his whole soul in prayer! And how lively is his nature in every grace of prayer! How deep his humility! How fervent his desires! How importunate his pleadings! How warm and hearty his thanksgiving!

And we need always to maintain upon our spirits a deep sense of the evil of sin, of our desert of death, of the dreadful holiness of God, and of the impossibility of our communication with him without a mediator, so that the name of Jesus may be ever precious to us, and so that we may never venture into the presence of God in set and solemn prayer without the eye of our soul to Christ, our glorious introducer.

DIRECTION 5: *Maintain always a praying disposition, a temper of mind ready to converse with God.*

This will be one way to keep all praying graces ever ready for exercise. Often and upon all occasions, visit him with whom you would obtain immediate communion at solemn times of devotion. Make the work of prayer your delight, and do not rest satisfied till you find pleasure in it.

Whatever advantages and opportunities you enjoy for social prayer, do not neglect praying in secret. At least once a day, constrain the business of life, to allow you to say something to God alone.

When you join with others in prayer and you are not the speaker, let your heart be kept intent and watchful to the work, that you may pray so much the better when you are the mouth of others to God.

In the midst of your duties in the world, take frequent occasion to lift up your heart to God. He is ready to hear a sudden sentence, and he will answer the breathings of a holy soul towards himself in the short intervals or spaces between your daily affairs. Thus you may pray without ceasing, as the apostle directs, and your graces may be ever active. If you make your addresses to God only in the morning and evening, and forget him all day, your heart will grow indifferent in worship; you will pay a salutation only with your lips and your knees and fulfil the task with dull formality.

DIRECTION 6: *Seek earnestly the assistance of the Holy Spirit.*

It is he that works every grace in us and fits us for every duty; it is he that awakens sleeping graces into activity; it is he that draws the soul near to God and teaches us this communication with heaven. He is the Spirit of grace and supplication; but because this is the subject of the following chapter, I shall pursue it no further here.

CHAPTER 4

The Spirit of Prayer

A ll the rules and directions that have been laid down in order to teach us to pray will be in-effectual if we have no divine aids. We are not sufficient of ourselves to think one thought, and all that is good comes from God. If we wish to attain the gift or grace of prayer, we must seek both from heaven. And since the mercies of God of this kind that are bestowed on men are usually attributed to the Holy Spirit, he may very properly be called the Spirit of prayer; as such his assistance is to be sought with diligence and importunity.

I confess, the spirit of prayer in our language may some-times signify a temper of mind well equipped and ready for the work of prayer. So when we say that there was a greater spirit of prayer found in churches in former days than now, we mean that there was a greater degree of the gift and grace of prayer found amongst men; their hearts and their tongues were better furnished and fitted for this duty. But to deny the spirit of prayer in all other senses, and declare that there is no need of any influences from the Holy Spirit to assist us to pray, carries in it a high degree of self-sufficiency and borders upon profaneness.

My task in this chapter shall be first to prove by plain and easy arguments that the Spirit of God does assist his people in prayer, then to show what his assistances are and how far they extend, that we may not expect more from him than Scripture promises nor attribute too little to his influences. And after a few cautions laid down, I shall give some directions on how the aids of the Holy Spirit may be obtained.

Proofs of the Assistance of the Spirit of God in Prayer

THE PROOFS WHICH I SHALL USE to demonstrate the influences of the Spirit of God in prayer are these: i. express texts of Scripture; ii. collateral texts; and iii. the experience of Christians.

I. THE FIRST ARGUMENT is drawn from such express texts of Scripture as these:

1. 'I will pour out on the house of David, and upon the inhabitants of Jerusalem, the spirit of grace and of supplications' (*Zech.* 12:10). Here the Holy Spirit of God is called a Spirit of supplication with respect to the special operations and ends for which he is here promised. The plentiful communication of his operations to men is often expressed by pouring him out upon them (*Isa.* 44:3; *Prov.* 1:23; *Titus* 3:6, and many other places). Now that this prophecy refers to the times of the gospel is evident, because the effect of it is a looking to Christ as pierced or crucified. 'They shall look on him whom they have pierced.'

OBJECTION: Some will say this promise refers only to the Jews at the time of their conversion.

ANSWER: Most of these exceeding great and precious promises that relate to gospel times are made expressly to Jacob, Israel, Jerusalem and Zion, in the language of the Old Testament. And how dreadfully should we deprive ourselves, and all the Gentile believers, of all these gracious promises at one stroke by such a confined exposition! The Apostle Paul sometimes takes occasion to quote a promise of the Old Testament made to the Jews and applies it to the Gentiles, as, 'I will dwell in them, and walk in them; and I will be their God, and they shall be my people . . .' (*2 Cor.* 6:16–18), which is written for the Jews (*Lev.* 26:12). 'Come out from among them; touch no unclean thing; and I will be a father to you' are taken from Isaiah 52:11 and Jeremiah 31:1, 9, where Israel alone is mentioned. And yet in 2 Corinthians 7:1 the apostle says, 'Having therefore these promises, dearly beloved, let us cleanse ourselves.' And thus he makes the Corinthians, as it were, possessors of these very promises.

He also gives us much encouragement to do the same when he tells us, 'Whatsoever things were written aforetime were written for our learning, that we through patience and comfort of the scriptures might have hope' (*Rom.* 15:4). And he assures us (verses 8–9) that Jesus Christ confirms the promises made to the fathers, that the Gentiles may glorify God for his mercy.

Again: 'All the promises of God in him are yea, and in him Amen, unto the glory of God' (*2 Cor.* 1:20). Now it would have been to very little purpose to have told the Romans or the Corinthians of the stability of all the promises of God, if their faith might not embrace them.

We are said to be blessed with faithful Abraham if we are imitators of his faith (*Gal.* 3:29). If we are Christ's, then are we Abraham's seed, and heirs according to the promise; heirs by faith of the same blessings that are promised to Abraham and to his seed (*Rom.* 4:13). Now this very promise, the promise of the Spirit, is received by us Gentiles as heirs of Abraham (*Gal.* 3:14), that the blessing of Abraham might come on the Gentiles through Jesus Christ, that we might receive the promise of the Spirit through faith. Having an interest therefore in his covenant, we have a right to the same promises, so far as they contain grace in them, that may be properly communicated to us. And therefore the house of David, in this prophecy of Zechariah, not only signifies the natural descendants of David the king, but very properly includes the family of Christ, the true David – believers that are his children, inhabitants of Jerusalem, and members of the true church, whether they were originally Jews or Gentiles. For in Christ Jesus men are not known by these distinctions; there is neither Jew nor Greek (*Gal.* 3:28).

2. In Luke 11:13, after Christ had answered the request of his disciples and taught them how to pray by giving them a pattern of prayer, he recommends them to ask his Father for the Holy Spirit, for a fuller and further assistance and instruction in this work of prayer, as the whole context seems to intimate.

3. 'The Spirit helpeth our infirmities: for we know not what we should pray for as we ought: but the Spirit itself maketh intercession for us with groanings which cannot be uttered' (*Rom.* 8:26). This cannot be interpreted as though the Holy Spirit assumed the work of Christ, who is our proper intercessor and advocate. For the Spirit, not being clothed with human nature, cannot properly be represented under such an inferior character, as the nature of prayer or petition seems to imply, whereas our Lord Jesus Christ, being man as well as God, may properly assume the character of a petitioner. The business of the Holy Spirit, therefore, is to teach and help us to plead with God in prayer for the things which we want. And this will appear evident by the next Scripture.

4. 'God hath sent forth the Spirit of his Son into your hearts, crying, Abba, Father' (*Gal.* 4:6). That is, the Spirit of God inclines and teaches us to address God in prayer as our Father. And so it is explained. 'Ye have received the Spirit of adoption, whereby we cry, Abba, Father' (*Rom.* 8:15). It may be noted here that this Spirit of adoption belongs to every true Christian in more or less degrees, otherwise the apostle's reasoning would not appear strong and convincing. 'Because ye are sons, he hath sent forth the Spirit of his Son,' etc.

5. 'Praying always with all prayer and supplication in the Spirit, and watching thereunto with all perseverance' (*Eph.* 6:18). These words *en pneumati* ('in the Spirit') have reference to the work of the Spirit of God in us, for so the words signify in other places of the New Testament: 'I cast out devils by the Spirit of God' (*Matt.* 12:28); 'he came by the Spirit into the temple' (*Luke* 2:27); 'to one is given by the Spirit the word of wisdom; to another the word of knowledge by the same Spirit' (*1 Cor.* 12:8–9). In this verse of the epistle to the Ephesians, it cannot properly signify praying with our own spirit, that is, with the intention of our own minds, because that seems to be implied in the next words, 'watching thereunto'.

OBJECTION: Some will say still that this praying in the Spirit was to be performed by an extraordinary gift which was communicated to the apostles and many others in the first age of Christianity: something like the gift of tongues at Pentecost, and various gifts among the Corinthians, when they prayed, preached, and sang by inspiration (*1 Cor.* 14).

ANSWER: Whatever there were of extraordinary and miraculous communications of the Spirit in those first days of the gospel, we do not profess to the same now. But the assistances of the Spirit of which we speak are in some measure attainable by Christians in all ages, for in this verse (*Eph.* 6:18), praying in the Spirit is enjoined to all believers, and at all times, with all sorts of prayer. Now it is not to be supposed that at all times and in all sorts of prayer Christians should have this extraordinary gift.

We may also further remark that the gift of prayer itself is not expressed as such an extraordinary and miraculous gift either in the prophecy of Joel 2, or in Acts 2, where that prophecy is fulfilled. Nor is it mentioned specifically among the miraculous gifts of the Holy Spirit, in those places where they are enumerated in the epistles of St Paul. But only the gift of prayer in an unknown tongue seems to be spoken of in 1 Corinthians 14, which refers rather to the gift of tongues than to that of prayer. And it is not unlikely that the omission or silence of the gift of prayer in those texts might be designed for this very purpose: namely, that though there were gifts of prayer by immediate inspiration in those days, there should be no bar laid against the expectations of Christians in all ages of some divine assistances in prayer, by a pretence that this was an extraordinary gift only to the apostles and the first Christians.

6. 'The "effectual fervent prayer" of a righteous man.' This is the way we translate James 5:16. In the original it is *deesis energoumene,* the 'inwrought' prayer. This word is used to describe persons possessed with a good or evil spirit, and it signifies here prayer wrought in us by the good spirit that possesses us, that leads and guides us. The word is used in this sense several times in 1 Corinthians 12, where the gifts of the Holy Spirit are spoken of. Yet let it be observed that here the apostle is speaking of an inwrought prayer that all Christians might be capable of,

for his epistle is directed to all the scattered tribes of Israel (*James* 1:1). And he tells them all to confess their faults to one another and pray for one another, that they might be healed, and for this reason: because the inwrought prayer of the righteous availeth much.

7. 'Praying in the Holy Ghost, keep yourselves in the love of God' (*Jude* 20–21). Now this epistle is written to all that are sanctified by God the Father, preserved and called in Jesus Christ (verse 1). They are all directed to pray by the assistance of the Holy Ghost. And those who do not have this Spirit are said to be sensual (verse 19).

I confess, the Holy Spirit has been in a great measure so long departed from his churches that we are tempted to think that all his operations in exhortation, in prayer, and preaching, belong only to the first age of Christianity and to the extraordinary ministers, prophets and apostles. It was from this absence of the Spirit that men proceeded to invent various methods to supply the absence of him in prayer, by paternosters, beads, litanies, responses and other forms, some good and some bad, to which they confined the churches, to keep up the form of worship and the attention of the people. At best, we are left by many teachers to the use of our mere natural powers, reason and memory. And from all this spring those reproachful expressions about the Spirit of prayer, and the endless labours of men to make this word signify only the temper and disposition of the mind. So the Spirit of adoption, in their sense, is nothing but a childlike temper, and the Spirit of prayer means nothing else but a praying frame of heart.

But since some texts speak expressly of the Holy Spirit as working these things in us, and since in many scriptures the Spirit of God is promised to be given us, to dwell and be in us, and to assist in prayer, why should we industriously exclude him from the hearts of the saints and thrust him out of those scriptures in which the words will possibly endure any other sense? It is, in my opinion, much more natural and reasonable for us to interpret the places in which the Spirit is mentioned according to the plain language of clear texts where the name of God's own Spirit is written.

However, if a man will but allow the Spirit of God and his assistances in prayer to be mentioned in any one text of Scripture so as to be persuaded and encouraged to seek those assistances that he may pray better, I will not be angry with him if he cannot find this Spirit in every text where others believe he is spoken of and designed.

II. THE SECOND ARGUMENT for the aids of the Holy Spirit in prayer is drawn from collateral scriptures: all those texts which represent the blessed Spirit as the spring of all that is good in us, and show us that all other duties of the Christian life are to be performed in and by this Holy Spirit.

Saints are born of this Spirit (*John* 3:6); are led by the Spirit (*Rom.* 8:14); walk in the Spirit (*Gal.* 5:16); live in the Spirit (*Gal.* 5:25); and by this Spirit mortify the deeds of the body (*Rom.* 8:13). The Spirit convinces of sin (*John* 16:9) and fits us for confession. The Spirit witnesses with our spirits that we are the children of God (*Rom.* 8:16) and thereby fills us with thanksgiving. The Spirit sanctifies us and fills us with love, faith, humility and every grace that is needed in the work of prayer. Why then should men take such pains to hinder us from praying by the Spirit, when it is only by this Spirit we can walk with God and have access to God (*Eph.* 2:18)?

III. THE THIRD ARGUMENT to prove that the Spirit of God sometimes assists men in the work of prayer is the experience of all Christians with regard to the grace of prayer, and many Christians in the use of the gift of it, too. The great difference between some believers and others in this respect, even where their natural abilities are equal, and the difference in believers themselves at different times, seems to denote the presence or absence of the Holy Spirit. Some persons at some special times will break out into a divine rapture in prayer and be carried far beyond themselves. Their thoughts, their desires, their language and everything that belongs to their prayer seems to have something of heaven in it.

I will allow that in some persons this may be ascribed to a great degree of understanding, intelligence, sensitivity, memory, natural inclinations of the mind, and fluency of the tongue. But many times also it shall be observed that those persons who have this gift of prayer do not exceed or equal their neighbours in sensitivity, intelligence, passion or eloquence. They may even be persons of very low abilities and below the common capacity of mankind.

Nor can it be always imputed to an overflow of animation and warm imagination, for this happens sometimes when they find their natural spirits not raised or exalted, but labouring perhaps under decline and great distress, and they can hardly speak or think about common affairs. I wish these testimonies to the aids of the Holy Spirit were more frequent amongst us.

REFLECTION: And it may be remarked that those who despise this gift of the Holy Spirit will deride the persons who profess to any share of it as foolish, stupid, ignorant wretches, and will represent them generally as unlearned, dull and unthinking creatures. And yet when the objection is made, From where does this fluency come, this fervour, and this wonderful ability of pouring out the soul before God in prayer, which the scoffers themselves cannot imitate? Oh! then it is attributed to our wit, our memory, our inventiveness, our sensitivity, our fervour, our confidence, or impudence – to anything rather than to the Spirit of God, because they are resolved to oppose his power and deny his work in the hearts of believers.

I might here, to confirm the doctrine of the aids of the Holy Spirit in our religious performances, add citations from the Articles and liturgy of the Church of England: 'We have no power to do good works, pleasant and acceptable to God, without the grace of God by Christ preventing us, that we may have a good will, and working with us when we have that good will' (*Art.* 10). 'The working of the Spirit – drawing up the mind to high and heavenly things' (*Art.* 17). And this ordinary work of the Holy Spirit in all believers, is called the 'inspiration of the Holy Spirit' (*Art.* 13).

'O God from whom all holy desires, all good counsels, and all just works do proceed'; and a little after:'Almighty God, who hast given us grace to make our common supplications' (*Second Collect at Evening Prayer*).And:'Grant that by thy inspiration we may think those things that be good, and by thy merciful guiding may perform the same' (in the *Collect, the Fifth Sunday after Easter*). Again: 'Almighty God, of whose only gift it cometh that thy faithful people do unto thee true and laudable service' (*13th Sunday after Trinity*).'Grant that thy Holy Spirit may in all things direct and rule our hearts' (*19th Sunday after Trinity*).

Homily 16th, pages 1–2, asserts the 'secret and mighty working of God's Holy Spirit which is within us: for it is the Holy Ghost, and no other thing, stirring up good and godly motions in their hearts.' Many more expressions of this kind might be collected from the *Homilies* and public prayers of the Church of England, so one would think none of that communion should throw reproach and scandal upon the assistances of the Holy Spirit in good works and religious duties.

How the Spirit Assists Us in Prayer

IT IS EVIDENT, then, that there is such a thing as the assistance of the Spirit of God in the work of prayer. But how far this assistance extends is a further subject of inquiry. And it is very necessary to have a proper notion of the nature and bounds of this divine influence, that we may neither expect more than God has promised, nor sit down negligently contented without such assistance as may be attained.

Persons in this, as in most other, cases are very ready to run away with extremes. They attribute either too much or too little to the Holy Spirit.

In my judgement, these are the persons who attribute too little to the Spirit of prayer:

i. Those who say that assistance is to be expected no more in prayer than in any ordinary and common affair of life. For example, when a ploughman breaks the clods of his ground and casts in the wheat and the barley, God instructs him to discretion and teaches him (*Isa.* 28:24–26). But this is, in effect, to deny his special influences.

ii. Those who allow the Spirit of God merely to excite some holy stirrings in the heart while they pray, and to awaken something of grace into exercise according to the words of a prayer; but say that he does nothing towards our obtaining the ability or gift of praying, nor at all assists us in the use of the gift with proper content, method or expression.

I am persuaded that the scriptures cited in the previous section concerning praying in the Spirit can never be explained this way in their full meaning. And I hope to make it apparent in this section that the Holy Spirit has more hand in prayer than both these opinions allow.

I think also, on the other hand, that these persons expect too much from the Spirit in our day:

i. Those who wait for all their inclinations to pray from immediate and present dictates of the Spirit of God, and who will never pray but when the Spirit moves them. I find in Scripture frequent exhortations to pray and commands to pray always, that is, to pray upon all occasions. Yet I find no promise or encouragement to expect that the Holy Spirit will, by sudden and immediate impulses in a perceptible way, dictate to me every time of prayer. For though the Spirit of God should sometimes withdraw himself in his influences, my duty and obligation to constant prayer still remain.

ii. Those who expect such aids of the Holy Spirit as to make their prayers the proper work of inspiration, such as the prayers of David, Moses and others recorded in Scripture. Let us not persuade ourselves that these workings of the Holy Spirit in ministers, or in common Christians while they teach or exhort or pray, arise to the character of those miraculous gifts that were given to the apostles and primitive believers, such as those described in the church of Corinth and elsewhere. For at those times a whole sermon, or a whole prayer together, was a constant impulse of the Holy Spirit, perhaps for the words as well as all the content of it, which made it truly divine. But in our own prayers the Spirit of God leaves us much to ourselves, to mingle many weaknesses and defects with our duties in the content, in the manner, and in the words; so we cannot say of one whole sentence that it is the perfect or the pure work of the Spirit of God. And we should run the danger of blasphemy to entitle the Spirit of God to everything that we speak in prayer, as well as to exclude all his assistance from all the prayers of the saints in our day.

iii. Those who hope for such influences of the Spirit as to render their own study and labours needless, and who, upon presumption of those divine impulses, have never given diligence to equipping themselves in a rational way with an ability to pray. Nor upon any occasion will they premeditate beforehand but rush upon the duty, as Peter went out at Christ's command to walk upon the water, and hope to be upheld and carried through all the duty without their own forethought. They will cite the text which was given to the disciples, 'When they deliver you up, take no thought how or what ye shall speak: for it shall be given you in that same hour what ye shall speak' (*Matt.* 10:19).

But this text has quite another purpose. It may be asked whether this word of Christ forbids them all premeditation, or only an anxious and troubled fear and care; just as we are told to take no thought for tomorrow (*Matt.* 6:34); that is, to be not overworried or disquieted about provision for tomorrow. But if Christ did utterly forbid them all preparation, still that command and promise to the apostles in miraculous times, when they should appear before magistrates, can never be given to encourage the sloth and laziness of every common Christian in our day when he appears in worship before God.

Now in order to find the happy medium between these two extremes, of attributing too much or too little to the Spirit of prayer, I have diligently consulted the Word of God. And so far as I am able to judge or determine, his assistance in prayer may be reduced to the following particulars:

1. *He bestows upon us our natural capacities,* some degree of understanding, judgement, memory, intelligence and natural temperament; some measure of confidence and fluency of speech; and readiness to utter the conceptions of our mind. This he does for believers in common with other men, for every good gift comes from God (*James* 1:17). And in a particular manner, the third person of the Trinity, the Holy Ghost, is generally represented as the agent in such sorts of operations, especially where they relate to religion.

2. *He blesses our diligence in reading, hearing, meditation, study and attempts of prayer,* by which, while we attend to useful rules and instructions, we treasure up a store of material for this duty and learn by degrees to express our thoughts with propriety and decency, to our own and others' edification.

Thus, in order to grow in the knowledge of the things of God as Christians, he adds a blessing to our studies: in the learning of tongues to interpret Scripture, and in the holy skill of exhortation, in order to become able ministers. All these are called spiritual gifts because, as has been shown, in the primitive times they were given suddenly and in an extraordinary manner, without laborious study to acquire them. But in our day these are to be obtained and developed by labour and use, by repeated trials, by time and experience, and the ordinary blessing of the Spirit of God.

The same must be said concerning the gift of prayer. He sanctifies our memory, to treasure up those parts of the Holy Scripture that are proper to be used in prayer; he makes it faithful to retain them and ready to recall them at proper times. If men become skilful in any faculty, and especially that which belongs to religion, it is justly attributed to God and his Spirit. For if he teaches the ploughman to manage wisely in sowing and reaping (*Isa.* 28:26–29), much more does he teach the Christian to pray.

He gives to everyone what gifts he pleases and works according to his good pleasure (*1 Cor.* 12:4–11). All secondary helps and means, when well attended to and well applied, are made successful by his powerful benediction. And we may say to those Christians who have the greatest gifts in prayer, Who made thee to differ from another? or what hast thou, that thou didst not receive? (*1 Cor.* 4:7). For if we live not by bread alone, but by every word of power and blessing that proceeds from the mouth of God (*Matt.* 4:4), much more may we say concerning the spiritual improvements of the mind that they are not attained by our labour alone, but by the good Spirit of God making our labour prosperous.

3. *He inclines our hearts to pray* and keeps them intent upon the work. By nature there is in all men an estrangement from God, and there is too much of it remaining in the best. There is a natural reluctance to the duties of immediate communion with God and a weariness in them. It is only the Spirit of God that works a heavenly disposition in us, that makes us ready to pray always, that stimulates us to take occasion from the many concerns of our souls or the affairs of life to go to the mercy-seat and abide there. It is he that kindly and secretly suggests,

Now is the accepted time. The Spirit says to the soul secretly, Seek my face; and the soul replies, Thy face, Lord, will I seek (*Psa.* 27:8). The Spirit says, Come to God by prayer, as well as to Christ by faith (*Rev.* 22:17). It is he that enlarges the desires towards God and gives silent intimations of hearing and acceptance. By his good stirrings he overcomes our delay and answers the carnal objections of our sinful and slothful hearts. He gives our spirits liberty for the work, as well as in it, and recalls our thoughts when wandering from God in worship, whether they be drawn away by our eyes, or our ears, or our busy imaginings, or the suggestions of the evil one.

It is the Holy Spirit who holds us to the duty in opposition to all discouragement, and makes us to wrestle and strive with God in prayer, to pour out our hearts before him, and to stir up ourselves to take hold of him, in agreement with the words of Scripture (*Gen.* 32:24; *Rom.* 15:30; *Psa.* 62:8; *Isa.* 64:7). The means which the Spirit of God generally uses to bring us to prayer and keep us to the duty is by working in our souls a lively sense of the necessity and advantage of it, or giving us some refreshment or delight in and by it.

And if, when we are engaged in our worldly affairs or in divine worship, the devil is permitted by sudden violent impressions on the imagination, to draw our hearts away to sinful objects, why should it be counted a strange thing that the blessed Spirit should cast in holy stirrings and encouragements to the duty?

4. *He often, by his secret teachings, supplies us with the content for prayer.* This is the express language of Holy Scripture (*Rom.* 8:26). 'The Spirit helpeth our infirmities: for we know not what we should pray for as we ought: but the Spirit itself maketh intercession for us' – and that

according to the mind or will of God (verse 27). All the senses that the wit of man has contrived to put upon this scripture to exclude the work of the Spirit of God, to make them signify anything else, are very much forced and strained.

It is plain that we do not know what is good for ourselves (*Eccles.* 6:12), and we of ourselves often ask for things hurtful to us (*James* 4:3). We are not acquainted with our own needs or the method of our relief. It is the Spirit that must convince us of sin and righteousness – of our sin, and the righteousness of Christ (*John* 16:9–10). He is a Spirit of illumination in all the affairs of religion. It is he alone that searches the deep things of God, that knows what God has prepared for believers (*1 Cor.* 2:9). And therefore he makes intercession, or teaches us to pray for things agreeing with the divine will and purpose.

He now and then also gives a hint of some argument to plead with God, either the name or mediation of Christ or some of his own promises in the gospel; for he is promised to take of the things of Christ and show them to us (*John* 14:26; 16:13–15). It is he that brings divine things to our remembrance, things that are suited to the various parts of prayer. He sets the glory and the majesty of God before our eyes, and supplies us with reason for adoration. By bringing sin to our remembrance, he fits us for confession; and by causing us to reflect on our many mercies, he richly supplies us with thanksgiving.

Now, since the evil spirit is said to pluck the good seed of the Word of God out of the heart (*Matt.* 13:19), why may we not suppose that the good Spirit puts good thoughts into the heart to prepare and equip us for such a duty as prayer? And such kinds of influences as these are called the good stirrings of the Spirit of God, which Christians of almost every sect and persuasion will allow in some degree.

5. *When the Spirit of God supplies us largely with content in prayer, he in some measure influences the method, too.* Method is but the arrangement of the materials of a prayer one after another. As it is impossible for our tongues to speak all these together, so it is impossible for our minds to receive all the kind hints of them from the Spirit at once; but they are received successively one after another, as seems good to him.

Sometimes he fills our souls with so deep and penitent a sense of our past sins that we break out before God into humble confessions in the very beginning of prayer: 'O Lord I am vile; what shall I answer thee? Mine iniquities are gone over my head, and the number of them is infinite.' And perhaps the soul dwells upon its humiliations through almost all the time of worship.

At another time the Spirit works as the Spirit of joy and thanksgiving, and the first words the lips utter are the language of gratitude and praise: 'I thank thee, Father, Lord of heaven and earth, that though the mysteries of the gospel are hidden from the wise and prudent, yet thou hast revealed them unto babes.'

Sometimes the soul is so inflamed with desire after such a particular grace, or mortification of some special sin, that almost from every part of prayer, adoration, confession, thanksgiving, etc., it will find some argument for bestowing that mercy and at every turn insert that special petition, enforcing it with new arguments and pleadings.

Thus, though the fine connection of one sentence with another, and the smooth and easy transition from one part of prayer to another, are left much to ourselves, the mere order of those materials will be in some degree under his direction or influence. And if we may understand those words of Elihu in a literal sense (*Job* 37:19), we need assistance in content, method and everything when we speak to God, and may well cry out, 'Lord, teach us what we should say to thee, for we cannot order our speech by reason of darkness. We need light and instruction from thee to frame our speeches and to put them in order.'

6. *The Spirit may be said to give some assistance also toward apt and proper expression in prayer.* For he concurs in an ordinary way to the use of our natural and acquired faculties of knowledge, memory, vivacity of spirit, fluency of speech, and holy confidence by which we express those thoughts in a becoming manner which he has aroused in us. This he does in preaching and conferring upon the things of God, and this more eminently in the work of prayer, so that a believer is able at some times to pour out his soul before God with a fullness of thought and variety of expression, to the great comfort of his own soul and the edification of his fellow worshippers. St Paul speaks of this boldness and utterance as a spiritual gift (*1 Cor.* 1:5; *2 Cor.* 8:7), and he often prayed for this confidence and freedom of speech in preaching (*Eph.* 6:19; *Col.* 4:3–4). We also have reason to ask it of God in prayer. For it is as necessary in that duty for carrying on the work of grace in our hearts and the building up of the church, the body of Christ, for which all gifts are given.

I might add that as the Holy Spirit frequently by secret hints supplies us with the content of prayer, he by that very means assists us toward expression, for expression is but the clothing of our thoughts or ideas in proper words. Now in this state in which the soul and body are so united, most of the ideas and conceptions of our mind are so joined to words that words arise, as it were, mingled with those ideas or conceptions which the Holy Spirit awakens within us. And we may humbly hope that when he has given us some secret whispers what we should pray for, he will enable us at least as much to use proper expressions that may convey the same thoughts to those who join with us in worship.

Especially when proper materials of prayer are brought to our mind in Scripture expressions, in some sense these are words taught by the Holy Ghost, that Spirit which is promised to bring to our remembrance those things which Christ has taught us. But this is more evidently so at the time, when, together with these expressions, the graces of prayer are wrought up to a vigorous activity, which is the next step of the assistance of the Spirit.

7. *He enlivens those graces in us which are suited to the duty of prayer.* He spiritualizes our natural inclinations, fixes them on proper objects, and enlarges and heightens their activity. When sin is recollected, he awakens anger, shame and sorrow. When God is revealed to the mind in his glory and justice, he overspreads the soul with holy awe and humble fear. When the Lord Jesus Christ and his redemption are upon the thoughts, the Holy Spirit warms and raises our desire and love.

We are in ourselves cold and dead to spiritual things; he makes us lively in prayer and holds us to the work. He begets a holy reverence of God while we adore him. He works in us delight in God and longing desires after him, fervency and importunity in our petitions for spiritual mercies, submission and resignation to the will of God in temporal things, faith in our Lord Jesus Christ and hope in the promises of the gospel, while we plead with God for an answer to our prayers. He fills us also with holy joy and exultation in God while we recall in prayer his glories or his benefits, and awakens all the springs of thankfulness.

As these qualities in their first operation are attributed to the Spirit of God (which it is not my present business to prove), so in their constant use in every duty they need his further assistance and efficacy, since of ourselves we are not sufficient for one good thought (2 *Cor.* 3:5), but all our sufficiency is of God. It is God of his good pleasure who works in us both to will and to do (*Phil.* 2:13). He gives us sincere aims and intents in our petitions; for in the character of our prayers, as well as the content, the assistance of the Spirit is necessary. That is hinted in the text before cited (*Rom.* 8:26): we do not know what to pray for as we ought, but the Spirit helps us. He influences our minds with a true and upright aim at the glory of God and our salvation. Otherwise we are ready to ask good things amiss, that we may spend them on our own selfish desires (*James* 4:3).

This work of the Spirit in awakening our graces, though I have mentioned it last, often begins before the prayer and precedes his other influences or our own labour in speaking to God.

Thus have I delivered broadly my sentiments concerning the extent of the influences of the Spirit of God in prayer and have shown how he qualifies us habitually for prayer, actually disposes and prepares us for it, and gives us present assistance in it. Lastly I would say that the most considerable and common assistance in prayer which is peculiarly attributed to the blessed Spirit as a Spirit of prayer and may be expected from him in our day, consists chiefly in these: putting our souls into a praying frame; stirring up holy desires after God; giving secret hints of our real needs and of arguments and promises to plead with God; and awakening the graces of love, fear, hope and joy that are suited to this duty. It is chiefly upon this account that he is called a Spirit of grace and supplication. When these are raised to a high degree, the heart will have a natural influence upon the thoughts, the memory, the language and the voice. Out of the abundance of the heart the mouth will speak. And for the most part the utterance will be proportional to the degree of inward devotion and to the natural and acquired abilities of the person that prays, except in some rare and glorious instances when men are carried beyond themselves by the uncommon presence of the divine Spirit.

Upon this subject I might venture to address those persons who will entertain nothing in religion but what appears to agree with principles of reason and philosophy, and yet have taken liberty to scoff at divine assistances in prayer. Let me entreat you, sirs, to tell me, what is there in this doctrine that is unreasonable to assert or unbecoming a philosopher to believe?

If the great God has required every man to pray, and will hear and reward the humble and sincere worshipper, why may we not suppose he is so compassionate as to help us in this work which he requires? Is he not full of goodness and ready to accept those sinners that return to him? And why shall not the same goodness incline him to assist those that desire and attempt to return? Why, when he sees the spirit willing and feeble, may he not by secret impressions draw out further the desires of that soul that already longs after him, and thus sweetly encourage the worship he delights in and prepare his servants for his own reward?

This address may be repeated with much more force and argument to Christians that profess the doctrine of the holy Trinity. Do you believe the Almighty God sent his own Son to teach us how to pray? And when we are taught the right way, why may not his own Spirit assist in the performance? Has Jesus Christ purchased heaven for us? And may not the Spirit be permitted to incline us to ask for that heaven and awaken our desires to seek it? When the Son of God saw us perishing in guilt and misery, did he descend and relieve and save us by dying for us?

And when the Spirit of God beholds a poor creature willing to receive this relief and salvation and yet is afraid to venture into the presence of an offended God, why may he not give secret hints of encouragement and draw out the addresses of the heart and lips to a God that is willing to pardon?

When he sees a humble sinner labouring and striving to break through temptations, to lay aside vain thoughts, to put carnal things far away from the mind and to converse with God alone, why may he not impress some divine thoughts upon him, stir up devout and strong devotion, make him surmount his difficulties, and raise him a little towards his heavenly Father? Since he has given him faculties of memory, invention and speech, why may he not assist those faculties when directed towards himself, and make them swifter and warmer in their advances toward God?

To what purpose is the blessed Spirit mentioned so often in the New Testament as one that helps forward the salvation of men? To what purpose does he sustain so many characters and offices in Scripture? And to what end is he so often promised to Christians, to be with them and dwell in them as a most glorious blessing of the gospel, if he is not permitted to do so much as this, in assisting men to draw near to their Maker and helping the children of God on earth to converse with their Father in heaven? Now if such condescensions as these are not unworthy of the blessed God, why should it be unworthy of a man or a Christian to believe them and hope for them?

Cautions about the Assistance of the Spirit

UPON THIS SUBJECT of the assistance of the Spirit of prayer, many practical cases arise in the thoughts of honest and pious persons. It is not my purpose here to enlarge in this way; but that I may prevent or obviate some difficulties, I would lay down these few cautions:

> CAUTION 1: *Do not believe that all manner of impulses or urgent impressions of the mind to go and pray proceed always from the blessed Spirit.*

Sometimes the mere terrors of conscience awakened under sense of guilt and danger will urge a natural man to go to prayer. So the sailors in Jonah's ship, when alarmed by a storm, all fell praying. The Spirit of God in his own operations makes much use of the consciences of men to carry on his own work; but when these inward impulses to pray arise merely from some frightening occurrence, or sudden conviction and torment of mind, and thus drag us into the presence of God without any assistance and strength to perform the duty, and without much regard to the success of the duty, we may justly fear the Holy Spirit of God does not have much hand in such impulses. For he both assists in the duty and makes us solicitous about the success of it. Sometimes Satan himself may so transform himself into an angel of light as to hurry and impel a person to go and pray. But his impulses are generally forceful and untimely. When we are engaged in some other business that is proper for that time, he tyrannically commands in a moment to leave all and go aside and pray.

But the Spirit of God draws us to God at a fit time, so as never to thrust out another necessary duty toward God or toward men. He is a God of order, and his Spirit always arouses to the proper duty of the hour, whereas Satan would but divert us from one business by forcing us away to another, and then leave us to our own weakness in it and vex us afterward with accusations.

CAUTION 2: *Do not expect the influences of the Spirit of prayer to be so intense and clear as to distinguish them with certainty from the stirrings of your own spirit.*

For the Spirit of God generally acts towards his people in accord with the dispensation which they are under, either in a more discernible or in a more imperceptible way.

Under the Old Testament, the Spirit of God often carried the prophets away as if in an ecstasy beyond themselves. Their style and gesture, as well as inward agitation of heart, were frequently different from the common manner of men, and sufficiently demonstrated to themselves, and in some measure to others also, that they were under the impressions of the Holy Spirit at special times.

Under the New Testament, the apostles had a more constant and habitual assistance of the Spirit, though it was extraordinary also. And in a calmer way they were influenced in prayer and preaching more in accord with rational nature, though without doubt they themselves well knew when they were under the certain conduct of the Holy Spirit.

In our day, when we have no reason to expect extraordinary inspirations, the Spirit of God usually leads us in so soft and silent a manner, amenable to the temper of our own spirits and circumstances of life, that his workings are not to be easily distinguished by ourselves or others from the rational doings of our own hearts influenced by moral arguments – though by the holy tendency and the sanctifying effects, we know we had some assistance from the blessed Spirit.

Such are his operations generally in conversion, sanctification and consolation. He works so naturally and sweetly with our own spirits that we cannot with certainty distinguish his working by any fervour or strength of impression. His working is best known by the favour and relish of divine things that we then feel in our souls, and by the consequent fruits of sanctification in our hearts and lives.

CAUTION 3: *Though we do not have any sure ground to expect extraordinary influences from the Spirit of prayer in our day, we ought not to deny them utterly, for God has nowhere bound himself not to bestow them.*

The chief ends for which immediate inspirations were given are long ceased among us where the gospel is so well established. Yet there have been instances in every age of some extraordinary testimonies of the Spirit of God to the truth of the gospel, both for conviction of unbelievers and for the instruction, encouragement and consolation of his own people.

In the conversion of a sinner, the Spirit's work is usually gradual, begun and carried on by providences, sermons, occasional thoughts and moral arguments, from time to time, till at last the man is become a new creature and resolves heartily to give up himself to Christ according to the encouragements of the gospel. Yet there are now and then some surprising and sudden conversions wrought by the over-powering influences of the Holy Spirit, something like the conversion of St Paul.

In the consolation of saints, the Spirit generally assists their own minds in comparing their hearts with the rule of the Word, and makes them to see that they are the children of God by finding the characters of adoption in themselves. This is his ordinary way of witnessing. But there are instances when the Spirit of God has in a more immediate manner spoken consolation and constrained the poor trembling believer to receive it; and this has been shown to be divine by the humility and advancing holiness that has followed.

So it is in prayer. The ordinary assistances of the Spirit given in our day to ministers or to private Christians in their utmost extent imply no more than what I have described in the foregoing chapter. But there are instances in which the Spirit of God has carried a devout person in worship far beyond his own natural and acquired powers in the use of the gift of prayer, and raised him to an uncommon and exalted degree of the exercise of praying graces, very near to those divine impulses which the primitive Christians enjoyed.

If a minister in a public assembly has been enabled to make his addresses to God with such a flow of divine eloquence, and spread the cases of the whole assembly before the Lord in such expressive language that almost everyone present has been ready to confess, 'Surely he knew all my heart'; if they have all felt something of a divine power attending his words, drawing their hearts near to the throne and giving them a taste of heaven; if sinners have been converted in numbers and saints made triumphant in grace and received blessed advances toward glory, I would not be afraid to say, 'Surely God is in this place, present with the extraordinary power and influence of his Spirit.'

If a Christian has been taught by this Spirit making intercession in him to plead with God for some particular mercy in such a rare strain of humble and heavenly argument that he has found in himself secret and inward assurances by something of a prophetic impulse that the mercy should be bestowed, and has never been mistaken; if grace has been in vigorous exercise in the prayer, and afterwards the success has always answered his expectation, I should not refrain from believing that the extraordinary presence of the Spirit of prayer was with him at that time. Dr Winter in Ireland, and several ministers and private Christians of the last age in Scotland, are notable and glorious instances of this gracious appearance of the Holy Spirit.

If a serious and humble worshipper who has been long seeking after the knowledge of some divine truth should find himself enlightened upon his knees with a beam of heavenly light shining upon that truth with most peculiar evidence, and teaching him more in one prayer than he had learned by months of labour and study, I should venture to acknowledge the immediate aids and answers of the Spirit of prayer and illumination. Luther is said to have enjoyed such divine favours at the Reformation of the church from popish darkness.

If a holy soul in conflict with doubts and fears has been waiting upon God in all his appointed ways of grace, seeking consolation and assurance of the love of God; if while he has been at the throne of grace, he has beheld God as his God, smiling and reconciled, and, as it were, has seen the work of God on his own heart in a bright and convincing light; and perhaps by some comfortable word of Scripture impressed on his thoughts has been assured of his love to God and the love of God to him; if from that immediate sensation of divine love he has been filled with joy unspeakable and full of glory as well as warmed with heavenly zeal for the honour of God, his God and Father, I must believe such a one to be sealed as a child of God by the sweet influence of the Spirit of adoption, teaching him to pray and cry, Abba, Father.

But because there have been many vain and foolish claims to such workings of the Spirit of God as these, I would make three remarks.

1. These are rare instances, bestowed by the Spirit of God in so sovereign and arbitrary a manner, according to the secret counsels of his own wisdom, that no particular Christian has any sure ground to expect them – though I am persuaded there are many more instances of them in secret among pious and humble souls than ever came to public notice.

2. They are best judged and distinguished from the mere effects of a warm notion, and from the spirit of delusion, not so much by the brightness and intensity of the present impression, as by their accordance with the standing rule of the Word of God and their influence towards humility and growing holiness. The same rule, therefore, judges the uncommon, as well as the common, assistances of this Spirit of supplication.

3. However near these rare and extraordinary impulses come to the inspiration of the apostles and first Christians

and we are sure the Spirit of prayer was with him. But great noise and vehement expressions may be used to make a show of fervency and power, with a purpose of making up for the lack of inward devotion. God himself was indeed present at Sinai with thunder and lightning and the sound of a trumpet once (*Exod.* 19). But another time when he came down to visit Elijah, he was not in the earthquake or in the tempest, but in the still small voice (*1 Kings* 19:11–12).

I would not impute the difference between the prayers of one minister and another, one Christian and another, merely to the presence or absence of the Holy Spirit. Natural constitutions, capacities, attainments, temperaments and providential circumstances can make a great difference. Nor would I impute the difference between the prayers of the same true Christians at different times only to the unequal assistances of the blessed Spirit, for many other things may concur to make them more or less cold or fervent, dull or lively, in the use of the gift of prayer.

Secondly, we may be in danger of mistake where there is but a small measure of the gift of prayer. How ready are some persons to judge that the Spirit of prayer is absent from the heart of the person who speaks to God, if he has but a mean and contemptible gift; if he seems to repeat the same things over again; if he labours under want of words or expresses his thought in improper or disagreeable language; if he has no beauty of connection between his sentences and has little order or method in the various parts of prayer!

Now, such persons that have so very small and despicable a talent should not be forward to speak in prayer in a great assembly or among strangers till by practice in a more private way they have attained more of this holy skill;

in the truth and power of them, they fall far short in the distinct evidence. For the Spirit of God has not taught us to distinguish any particular parts or paragraph of even an extraordinary prayer, so that anyone can say, These are perfect divine inspirations. This because he would have nothing stand in competition with his written Word as the rule of faith and practice of his saints.

CAUTION 4: *Do not make the gift of prayer the measure of your judgement concerning the Spirit of prayer.*

If we follow this rule, there are three cases in which we may be led into mistake.

The first case is when the gift is in great and lively use. Be careful of believing that all those persons who use very pious expressions with great seeming fervency and much fluency of speech, are praying by the Spirit; it may be that their behaviour and character in the world is sinful and abominable in the sight of God. It is true indeed, the Spirit of God sometimes bestows consider-able gifts upon persons that are unconverted. But we are not immediately to believe that everything that is bright and beautiful is the peculiar work of the Spirit in our day, unless we have some reason to hope the person is also one of the sons of God.

Much less can we suppose that noisy gesture, a distorted countenance, forcefulness and vociferation are signs of the presence of the divine Spirit. Sometimes indeed th extraordinary anguish of mind or inward fervour of emotion have prompted from the saints of God lou complaints and groanings. David sometimes practise this, as appears in his psalms. Jesus Christ himself, who pressed with sorrows heavier than man could bear, offer strong cries and tears in the days of his flesh (*Heb.* 5:

1

yet there may be much of the Spirit of prayer in the hearts of some persons as these. It may be they are young Christians lately converted and are but beginning to learn to pray. The business of praying is a new work to them, though their zeal is warm and their hearts alive in grace. And natural bashfulness may sometimes hinder the use of a good gift in prayer.

Or it may be they have very low natural abilities, a poor aptitude and memory, a barrenness of words, or some difficulty in expressing themselves about other affairs. They may be some of those foolish things of this world that God has called to the knowledge of his Son and filled their hearts with rich grace. But grace does not exalt nature so far as to change dullness and low capacity into a sprightliness of thought and vivacity of language.

Or perhaps they have long become unaccustomed to praying in public, and at first when they are called to it again may be much at a loss as to the gift of prayer, though grace may be in its advances in the soul.

Or perhaps they are in deep humility and mourning before God under a sense of guilt; or overwhelmed with fears of divine desertion; or battling and wrestling hard with some impelling temptation; or under a present depression of mind by some heavy sorrow; or may be as David when he was so troubled that he could not speak (*Psa.* 77:4).

Or finally, God may withhold from them the use of the gift of prayer to punish them with shame and confusion for some neglected duty, and chastise them, it may be, for carelessness in seeking after this holy skill of speaking to God; though some graces, such as zeal and love, may be at work in the heart.

Sometimes it may happen that the Spirit of prayer is communicated in a great degree to an humble Christian who falls into many thoughtless improprieties of gesture in prayer, or delivers his sentences with a most inappropriate tone of voice. Perhaps he was never taught proper decorum when he was young, and such ill habits are not easily cured afterward. We are not therefore to despise and be offended at all such prayers, but to endeavour to separate what is pious and divine from the human frailty and weakness, to pity such persons heartily, and be so much the more aroused ourselves to seek after everything that is agreeable in the gift of prayer.

Thirdly, we are in danger of mistake when the gift is not used at all. Some persons have been ready to imagine they could not pray by the Spirit except when they used the gift of prayer themselves. But this is a great mistake. For though one person is the mouth for the rest to God, every one that joins with him may be justly said to pray in the Spirit, if all the graces that are suited to the duty of prayer and its expressions are in lively vigour. And it is possible that a poor humble Christian may pray in the Spirit in the secret and silence of his heart, while the person that speaks to God in the name of others has very little or nothing of the Spirit of God with him, or when the words of the prayer are a known and prescribed form. Though the Spirit of prayer in the common language of Christians is never applied to the use of the gift where there is no grace, it is often applied to the use of the grace of prayer without any regard to the gift.

CAUTION 5: *Do not expect the same measure of assistance at all times from the Spirit of prayer.*

He has nowhere bound himself to be always present with his people in the same degree of influence, though he will never utterly forsake those whose heart he has taken possession of as his temple and residence. He is compared to the wind by our Lord Jesus Christ (*John* 3). The wind blows where and when it listeth. It is not always equal in the strength of its gales or constant in blowing on the same part of the earth. The Holy Spirit is a sovereign and free agent who dispenses his favours in what measure he pleases and at what times he will.

Those therefore who at present enjoy a large share of assistance from the Spirit of prayer should not presume that they shall always enjoy the same. Those that have in any measure lost it should not despair of recovering it again. And those who have not yet been blessed with his influences may humbly hope to attain them by seeking.

This naturally leads me to the following section.

Directions to Obtain and Keep the Spirit of Prayer

THE LAST THING I PROPOSE is to give some directions on how to obtain and to keep the assistance of the Holy Spirit:

DIRECTION 1: *Seek earnestly after converting grace and faith in Jesus Christ.*

For the Spirit of grace and of supplication dwells in believers only. He may visit others as he is the author of some spiritual gifts, but he abides only with the saints. The sons of God are so many temples of his Holy Spirit (*1 Cor.* 3:16), and he perfumes their souls with the sweet incense of prayer ascending up from their hearts to God who dwells in heaven. If we are in the flesh, that is, in an unconverted state, we cannot please God, or walk in the Spirit, or pray in the Spirit (*Rom.* 8:8–9). It is only the children of God who receive his Spirit as a Spirit of adoption (*Rom.* 8:15). Because you are sons, he has sent the Spirit of his Son into your hearts, and it is by faith in Christ Jesus that we receive this Spirit (*Gal.* 3:14). And wherever he is the Spirit of all grace, he will in some measure be a Spirit of prayer, too.

Let all Christians that would maintain and increase in the gifts of the Holy Spirit live much by the faith of the Son of God and be frequent in acts of dependence upon Christ Jesus. For the Spirit is given to him without measure and in all fullness, that from his fullness we may derive every gift and every grace (*John* 3:34; 1:16). As in the natural, so in the spiritual or mystical body, the spirits that give life and activity to the heart and tongue and all the members are derived from the head. He that lives in heaven as our intercessor and advocate to present our addresses and petitions to the throne will send his own Spirit down to earth to assist us in drawing them up. Live much upon him as your intercessor and your vital head.

> DIRECTION 2: *Give all diligence to acquire this gift or holy skill, according to the directions concerning the content, method and manner of prayer which have been laid down before; and be much in the practice of prayer, both in secret and with one another, that young habits may grow and be developed by use.*

The Spirit of God will come and bless the labours of the mind towards the acquiring of spiritual gifts. Timothy is commanded to give attendance to reading and meditation on the things of God, and to give himself wholly up to the work, that his profiting may appear to all, though he received gifts of inspiration (*1 Tim.* 4:13; cf. verses 14–15; 2 *Tim.* 1:6). And much more should we do it, who are not thus inspired.

Though prophecy was a gift of immediate inspiration, there were of old the schools of the prophets, or the college, in which young men were trained up in the study of divine things, that they might be the better prepared to receive the Spirit of prophecy and to use and develop it better. These were called the sons of the prophets (*2 Kings* 6:1; *2 Chron.* 34:22). St Paul laboured and strove with his natural powers while the Spirit worked mightily in him (*Col.* 1:29).

Do not imagine yourselves to be in danger of quenching the Spirit by endeavouring to equip yourselves with content or expressions of prayer, for the Spirit of God usually works in and by the use of means.

As in the things of nature, so in the things of grace, it is a true and divine proverb: 'The soul of the sluggard desireth, and hath nothing: but the soul of the diligent shall be made fat' (*Prov.* 13:4). We are to put forth our best efforts and then hope for divine assistance, for the Spirit of God helps together with us (*Rom.* 8:26), as when a man takes hold of one end of a burden to lift it and a mighty helper makes his labour effective by lifting it at the other end and fulfilling the intention.

It was the encouragement which David gave to his son Solomon: 'Arise and be doing, and the LORD be with thee' (*1 Chron.* 22:16). While we are stirring up ourselves to obey the command of God and seek his face, we have reason to hope his Spirit will strengthen us to this obedience and assist us in seeking. When God commanded Ezekiel to arise and stand upon his feet and to put forth his natural powers towards raising himself, the Spirit entered into him, set him upon his feet, and by a divine power made him stand (*Ezek.* 2:1–2).

DIRECTION 3: *Pray earnestly, and pray for the promised Spirit as a Spirit of prayer.*

Do not depend upon all your natural and acquired abilities, whatever glorious attainments you enjoy. How some persons have been shamefully disappointed when they have ventured presumptuously to make their addresses to God by the mere strength of their own wit and memory and confidence! What hurry and confusion of thought they have fallen into and been incapable of proceeding in the duty! The Holy Spirit shall be given to those who ask aright (*Luke* 11:13). Plead the promises of Christ with faith in his name (*John* 14:16–17). For he has promised, in his own name and in his Father's, to send his Holy Spirit.

DIRECTION 4: *Do not quench the Spirit of prayer by confining yourselves to any set forms whatever.*

Though the Spirit of God may be present and assist in the exercise of grace while we use forms of prayer, let us beware of stifling or restraining any good desires and heavenly devotions that are stirred up in our hearts when we pray. If we refuse to express them because we will not vary from the form that is written down before us, we run a great risk of grieving the Holy Spirit and causing him to depart from us, as he is the Spirit of grace. And we hinder ourselves from his assistance in the gift of prayer.

While you borrow the best aids in your devotion from those prayers that are composed by the Spirit of God in Scripture, take care not to quench his further operations by confining yourselves entirely to those words and expressions. The Holy Spirit may be quenched even by tying yourselves to his own words. For if he had thought those words of Scripture all-sufficient for all the intents and needs of his saints in prayer, he would have given some hint of it in his Word. He would have required us to use those prayers always, and there would have been no further promise of the Spirit's assistance in this work. But now he has promised it and has forbidden us to quench it while we pray without ceasing (*1 Thess.* 5:17, 19).

DIRECTION 5: *Do not dare to indulge yourselves in a course of spiritless worship, in a round of formality and lip-service, without pious dispositions and warm devotion in your own spirits.*

There may be danger of this formality and coldness in the use of the gift of prayer even when we are not tied to a form. How can we think the Spirit of God will come to our assistance if our spirits withdraw and are absent from the work?

Take notice of the frame of your minds in prayer; observe the presence or absence of this divine assistant, the Holy Spirit. And since we are told to pray always in the Spirit (*Eph.* 6:18), do not be satisfied with any prayer in which you have found nothing at all of inward divine stirrings towards God through the work of his own Spirit. O the dismal character and temper of those souls that spend whole years of worship, and multiply duties and forms of devotion without end and without number, with no Spirit in them.

DIRECTION 6: *Be thankful for every aid of the Spirit of God in prayer, and develop it well.*

Spread all the sails of your soul to make use of every gale of this heavenly wind that blows when and where it listeth (*John* 3:8). Comply with his holy stirrings. Abide in prayer when you feel your graces raised into a lively activity, for it is the Spirit that makes alive (*John* 6:63). He does not always come in an easily perceptible manner; therefore be tenderly careful, lest you shake him off or thrust him from the door of your hearts, especially if he is a rare visitor.

DIRECTION 7: *Beware of pride and self-sufficiency when at any time you feel great enlargements of soul, warm affections and divine delight in prayer.*

Do not attribute to yourselves what is due to God, lest he be provoked. The gift of prayer in lively and flowing activity will be in danger of puffing up the unwary Christian. But let us remember that it is with the humble that God will dwell (*Isa.* 57:15), and to the humble he gives more grace (*James* 4:6).

DIRECTION 8: *Do not grieve the Holy Spirit in the course of your life in the world.*

Walk in the Spirit, and ye shall not fulfil the lusts of the flesh, nor make him depart grieved (*Gal.* 5:16; *Eph.* 4:30). Heed the whispers of the Spirit of God when he convinces of sin, and comply with his secret dictates when he leads to duty, especially the duty of prayer, at fit times and seasons. Do not grieve him by your unwatchfulness or by wilful sins; do not resist him, lest he depart. But rather seek greater degrees of his enlightening and sanctifying influences.

If you thrust him utterly away from you in the world, he will not take it well at your hands or grant you his presence in your private devotions or in the church. If you grieve him before men, he will withdraw from you when you wish to come near to God, and leave your soul in grief and bitterness. Deal kindly with him when he comes to convict your conscience or to direct and incline you even to difficult and self-denying duties. Value his presence as a Spirit of knowledge and sanctification, and he will not forsake you as a Spirit of prayer. Live in the Spirit, walk in the Spirit, and then you shall also pray in the Spirit.

Thus have I given short and plain directions how the assistances of the Holy Spirit may be obtained, according to the encouragements of the Word of God and the experience of praying Christians. For though he is a sovereign and free agent, and his communications are of pure mercy so that we can claim no merit, the Spirit of God has condescended so far as to give promises of his own presence to those who seek it in the way prescribed.

I would not finish this section without a word of advice to those from whom the Spirit of prayer is in a great measure withdrawn, in order to their recovering his customary assistance.

1. *Be deeply aware of the greatness of your loss, mourn over his absence, and lament after the Lord.*

Recall the times when you could pour out your whole heart before God in prayer with a rich plenty of expressions and lively graces. Compare those shining hours with the dull and dark times which you now complain of. Go and mourn before your God, and say, 'How vigorous were all the powers of my nature before in worship! How warm my love! How fervent my zeal! How overflowing was my repentance, and how joyful my thanksgiving and praises! But now what a coldness has seized my spirit! How dry and dead is my heart, and how far off from God and heaven even while my knees are bowed before him in secret! How long, O Lord, how long before thou return again?' Beware of being satisfied with a circle and course of duties without the life, power and pleasure of religion. The Spirit of God will come and revisit the mourners. When God heard Ephraim bemoaning himself, he turned his face toward him with compassion (*Jer.* 31:18–20).

2. *Look back and notice the steps by which the Spirit of God withdrew himself, and search after the sins that provoked him to depart.*

He does not go away and leave his saints, except they grieve him.

See if you cannot find some sensual iniquity indulged. He hates this, for he is a Spirit of purity. David might well fear, after his scandalous sin, that God would take away his Holy Spirit from him (*Psa.* 51:11).

Recall whether you have not rushed upon some presumptuous sin and run counter to your own light and knowledge. This is a sure way to make him withdraw his favourable presence.

Ask your conscience whether you have not resisted this blessed Spirit when he has brought a word of conviction, command or reproof to your soul; whether you have not refused to obey some holy influence and been heedless of his kind stirrings in any duty or worship. This highly deserves his resentment and departure.

Reflect whether you have not sinfully neglected your prayer closet often; or often left it almost as soon as you came to it from a prevailing carnality of mind and sinful weariness of duty; or often shuffled off the work like a tiresome task because you fancied the world called you. It is no wonder then if the Spirit of prayer withdraws from your closet even when the world gives you liberty to go there. And you may expect also that if you decline secret prayer, the Spirit will not always attend you in public.

Consider whether you have not grown proud and vain in gifts and attainments and thus provoked the Holy Spirit to leave you to yourself, to show you your own weakness and insufficiency and to abase your pride.

Cry earnestly to him, and beg that he would reveal his own enemy, which has given him such just offence. And when you have found it out, bring it and slay it before the Lord. Confess the sin before him with deep humiliation and self-abasement. Abhor, renounce and abandon it forever. Bring it to the cross of Christ for pardon, and there let it be crucified and put to death. Cry daily for strength against it from heaven, renew your pledge to be the Lord's and to walk more watchfully before him.

3. *Remember how you obtained the Spirit of prayer at first. Read over the foregoing directions and put them all into practice afresh.*

Was it by faith in Christ Jesus that the Spirit was first received? Then by renewing acts of faith in Christ, seek his return. It is he who first gives and he who restores this glorious gift.

Was it in the way of labour, duty, and diligence that you found the Spirit's first assistance? Then stir up all the powers of your soul to the same diligence in duty, and strive and labour to get near to the throne of God with the utmost use of your natural abilities, depending on his secret influences and hoping for his response. If the wind does not blow, tug harder at the oar, and so make your way toward heaven. Do not dare to indulge a neglect of prayer upon pretence that the Spirit is departed, for without stirring up your soul to seek him, you cannot expect him to revisit you.

Was he at first given you more perceptibly as an answer to prayer? Then plead earnestly with God again to restore him. If he does not supply you with material for prayer by his special and present influences, take with you words from his own holy book and say to him, Take away all iniquity, and return and receive me graciously (*Hos.* 14:1–2). Plead with him his own promises made to returning backsliders (*Jer.* 3:22, *Ezek.* 36:25) and put him in mind of the repenting prodigal in the embraces of his father.

When you have found him, hold him fast and never let him go (*Song of Sol.* 3:4). Do not again indulge those follies that provoked his anger and absence. Receive his first appearances with great thankfulness and holy joy. Let him abide with you and maintain all his sovereignty within you; and see that you abide in him in all subjection. Walk humbly and sin no more, lest a worse thing befall you: lest he depart again from you and fill your spirit with fear and bondage and make you to possess the bitter fruit of your folly; lest he give you up to months and years of darkness, and that measure of the gift of prayer you had attained should be so imprisoned and bound up that you may be hardly able to pray at all.

CHAPTER 5

Persuasive Arguments to Learn to Pray

I t is to little purpose that the nature of prayer is explained, so many rules framed and directions given to teach persons this divine skill of prayer, if they are not persuaded of the necessity and usefulness of it. I therefore finish this work by leaving on the mind of the readers some persuasive arguments that this attainment is worth their seeking.

I am not going to address myself to persons who through a neglect of serious religion have risen to the insolence of scoffing at all prayers besides public divine services and authorized forms. Nor am I now seeking to persuade those who may have some taste of serious piety, but by a superstitious and obstinate veneration of liturgies, have forever abandoned all thoughts of learning to pray.

I think there is enough in the second chapter of this treatise to convince impartial men that the gift of prayer is no fanatical pretence, not the empty talk of a particular party, but a useful and necessary qualification for all: a piece of Christian skill to be attained in a rational way by the use of proper means and the blessing of the Holy Spirit. If what I have said cannot influence these persons, I leave them to the further instruction and reproof of a great and venerable man whose name I have mentioned before, a learned prelate of the Established Church, who speaks thus:

> For anyone to satisfy himself with a form of prayer is still to remain in infancy: It is the duty of every Christian to grow and increase in all the duties of Christianity, gifts as well as graces. Now how can a man be said to live suitable to these rules who does not put forth himself in some attempts and endeavours of this kind? And if it be a fault not to strive and labour after this gift, much more it is to jeer and despise it by the name of extempore prayer, and praying by the Spirit; which expressions, as they are frequently used by some men by way of reproach, are for the most part a sign of a profane heart and such as are altogether strangers from the power and comfort of this duty.

My business here is to address myself to those who have some sense of their obligation to prayer and of the impossibility of answering all their necessities by any set forms, but through a coldness and indifference in things of religion take no pains to acquire the gift, or content themselves with so slight and imperfect a degree of it that they or others are not much the better. It is this sort of Christian that I wish to stir up and awaken to diligence in seeking so valuable an attainment.

But here I would have it again observed that the qualification I recommend does not consist in a treasure of sublime notions, florid phrases and fine eloquence, but merely in a competent supply of religious thoughts, which are the fit materials of prayer, and a readiness to express them in plain and proper words with a free and natural decency.

1. THE FIRST ARGUMENT *I shall draw from the purpose and dignity of this gift: There is such a thing as correspondence with heaven, and prayer is a great part of it while we dwell on earth.*

Who would not be ambitious to correspond with heaven? Who would not be willing to learn to pray? This is the language in which God has appointed the sons of Adam, who are but worms and dust, to address the king of glory, their Maker. Shall there be any among the sons of Adam that will not learn this language? Shall worms and dust refuse this honour and privilege? This is the speech which the sons of God use in talking with their heavenly Father. Shall not all the children know how to speak it? This is the manner and behaviour of a saint, and these the expressions of his lips while his soul is breathing in a divine air and stands before God. Why should not every man be acquainted with this manner of address, that he may join in practice with all the saints and have access at all times to the greatest and the best of beings?

There are indeed some sincere Christians who daily worship God, and yet they are often labouring for want of matter and are perpetually at a loss for proper expressions: They have only a low attainment of this holy skill. But it is neither their honour nor their interest to perform so divine a work with so many human weaknesses, and yet be satisfied with them. There are children who can only cry after their father and stammer out a broken word or two by which he can understand their meaning. But these are ungrown infants. The father would rather see his children advancing to manhood and occupying themselves daily with that broad and free conversation with himself which he allows and to which he graciously invites them.

Prayer is a sacred and appointed means to obtain all the blessings that we want, whether they relate to this life or the life to come. Shall we not know how to use the means God has appointed for our own happiness? Shall so glorious a privilege lie unused through our own neglect?

If the business of prayer were nothing else but coming and begging mercy of God, it would be the duty of every man to know how to draw up such petitions and present them in such a way as becomes a mortal petitioner. But prayer is a work of much larger extent. When a holy soul comes before God, he has much more to say than merely to beg. He tells his God what a sense he has of the divine attributes, and what high esteem he pays to his majesty, his wisdom, his power and his mercy. He talks with him about the works of creation and stands wrapped up in wonder. He talks about the grace and mystery of redemption and is yet more filled with admiration and joy. He talks of all the affairs of nature, grace and glory; he speaks of his works of providence, of love and vengeance, in this and the future world. Infinite and glorious are the subjects of this holy communion between God and his saints. Shall we content ourselves with sighs and groans and a few short wishes, and deprive our souls of so rich, so divine, so manifold a pleasure, for want of knowing how to express such meditations and to speak this blessed language?

How excellent and valuable is this skill of praying, in comparison with the many inferior arts and accomplishments of human nature that we labour night and day to obtain! What toil do men daily undergo for seven years together, to acquire the knowledge of a trade and business in this present life! Now the greatest part of the business between us and heaven is transacted in the way of prayer. With how much more diligence should we seek the knowledge of this heavenly commerce than anything that concerns us merely on earth! How many years of our short life are spent to learn the Greek, Latin and French tongues, that we may communicate among the living nations or understand the writings of the dead? Shall not the language in which we converse with heaven and the living God be thought worth equal pains? How laboriously do some persons study the art of conversation, that they may be accepted in all company and share in the favour of men? Is not the same care due to seek all methods of acceptance with God, that we may approve ourselves in his presence? What a high value is set upon human oratory or the art of persuasion, by which we are equipped to debate and prevail with our fellow creatures? This art of divine oratory, which teaches us to utter our inward utterings of soul, and plead and prevail with our Creator through the assistance of the Holy Spirit and mediation of our Lord Jesus – is it of no esteem with us?

O let the excellency and high value of this gift of prayer engage our earnestness and endeavours in proportion to its superior dignity. Let us covet the best of gifts with the warmest desire, and pray for it with ardent supplications (*1 Cor.* 12:31).

2. ANOTHER ARGUMENT *may be borrowed from our very character and profession as Christians. Some measure of the gift of prayer is of great necessity and universal use to all who are called by the name.*

Shall we profess to be followers of Christ, and not know how to speak to the Father? Are we commanded to pray always upon all occasions, to be constant and fervent in it; and shall we be contented with ignorance and incapacity to obey this command? Are we invited by the warmest exhortations and encouraged by the highest hopes to draw near to God with all our needs and sorrows; and shall we not learn to express those needs and pour out those sorrows before the Lord? Is there a way made for our access to the throne by the blood and intercession of Jesus Christ; and shall we not know how to form a prayer to be sent to heaven and spread before the throne by this glorious intercession? Is his Holy Spirit promised to teach us to pray; and shall a Christian be careless or unwilling to receive such divine teachings?

No faculty in the whole Christian life is called into so frequent exercise as this. And it is most unfitting to be always at a loss to perform the work which daily necessity requires and daily duty demands. Will a person who cannot read profess to be a scholar? Shall any man that cannot preach claim to be a minister? It is but a poor pretence we make to Christianity if we are not able, at least in secret, to supply ourselves with a few meditations or expressions to continue a little in this work of prayer.

Remember then, O Christian: this is not a gift that belongs alone to ministers or to heads of families, who are under constant obligation to pray in public, though it most highly concerns them to be expert in this holy skill, that with courage and presence of mind, with honour and decency, they may discharge this part of their duty to God in their congregations and households. But this duty has a further extent. Every man that is joined to a church of Christ should seek after an ability to help the church with his prayers, or at least upon more private occasions to join with a few fellow Christians in seeking God their Father. Nor are women, though they are forbidden to speak in the church, forbidden to pray in their own families or with one another in private.

I am persuaded Christians would ask one another's assistance more frequently in prayer upon special occasions if a good gift of prayer were more commonly sought and more universally obtained. Nor would congregations where a minister is suddenly taken sick be dismissed and the whole Lord's Day pass without public worship, if some grave and prudent Christian of good ability in prayer would but take that part of worship upon him, together with the reading of some well-composed sermon and some useful portion of Holy Scripture. Doubtless this would be most acceptable to that God who loves the gates of Zion, or his own public ordinances, more than all the dwellings of Jacob, or worship of private families (*Psa.* 87:2).

This gift is necessary wherever social prayer may be performed. But the necessity of it reaches further still. There is not a man, woman or child capable of seeking God who is not bound to exercise something of the gift of prayer. And those that never have any call from providence to be the mouth of others in speaking to God are called daily to speak to God themselves. It is necessary, therefore, that every soul should be so equipped with a knowledge of the perfections of God as to be able to adore them distinctly; should be so acquainted with its own needs as to express them particularly before God, at least in the conceptions and language of the mind; should so apprehend the encouragements to pray as to be able to plead with God for supply; and should so observe and recall divine mercies as to repeat some of them before God with humble thanksgiving.

3. A THIRD ARGUMENT *is drawn from the divine delight and very great advantage of this gift to our own souls and to the souls of all that join in prayer with us.*

Christians, have you never felt your spirits raised from a carnal and vain temper of mind to a devout frame by a lively prayer? Have you not found your whole souls overspread with holy devotion and carried up to heaven with most abundant pleasure by the pious and regular performance of him that speaks to God in worship? And when you have been cold and indifferent to divine things, have you not felt that heavy and lifeless humour expelled by joining with the warm and stirring expressions of a person skilful in this duty? How sweet a refreshment have you found under inward burdens of mind or outward afflictions, when in broken language you have told them to your minister and he has spread them before God in such words as have expressed your whole souls and your sorrows? And you have experienced a sweet serenity and calmness of spirits; you have risen up from your knees no more sad-faced.

Have you not wished for the same gift yourselves, that you might be able upon all occasions to address the throne of grace and pour out all your hearts in this manner before your God? What a sad inconvenience it is to live in such a world as this, where we are liable daily to so many new troubles and temptations, and not be able to express them to God in prayer unless we find them written in the words of a form! And how hard it is to find any form suited to all our new needs and sorrows!

At other times what divine impressions of holiness have you felt in public worship in the congregation when this duty has been performed with holy skill and fervency, and in that prayer you have received more solid edification than from the whole sermon? How dead have you been to all sinful temptations, and how much devoted to God? Do you not long to be able to pray in this way in your households and in your own room? Would it not be a pleasure for men to be thus able to engage their whole families daily, and for Christians thus to engage one another when they meet to pray to their common God and Father and to help one another onward to the world of praise? When the disciples had just been witnesses of the devotion of our Lord (*Luke* 11:1), who spoke as man had never spoken, their hearts grew warm under the words of that blessed worshipper; and one of them, in the name of the rest, cried out, 'Lord, teach us to pray, too.'

Thus a good attainment of this gift is made a fitting instrument of sanctification as well as comfort, by the co-working power of the blessed Spirit.

But on the other hand, has not your painful experience sometimes taught you that zeal and devotion has been cooled and almost quenched by the vain repetitions or weak and wandering thoughts of some fellow Christian that leads the worship? And at another time a well-framed prayer of beautiful order and language has been rendered disagreeable by some inappropriate tones and gestures, so that you have been weary of listening and longed for the conclusion.

Who would willingly remain neglectful of attaining an instrument so sweet and successful in advancing religion in its powers and pleasures in their own hearts and the hearts of all men round about them?

4. THE HONOUR OF GOD AND THE REPUTATION OF RELIGION IN THE WORLD *will afford me another source of arguments to move you to attain this skill of prayer.*

The great God esteems himself dishonoured when we do not pay him the best worship we are capable of. The work of the Lord must not be done negligently. It is highly for his honour that we be furnished with the best talents for his service and that we employ them in the best manner. This reveals to the world the inward high esteem and veneration we have for our Maker; this gives him glory in the eyes of men. But to neglect utterly this gift of prayer, to serve him daily with a few sudden thoughts with rude and improper expressions that never cost us anything but the labour of our lips, is not the way to sanctify his name among men.

Sinful sloth and indifference in religion have tempted some men to believe that God is not an interested and exact inquirer into outward things. And if they can persuade themselves their intentions are right, they imagine that for the substance and form of their sacrifice, anything will serve. And as though he were not a God of order, they address him often in confusion. Because the heart is the chief thing in divine worship, like some foolish Israelite, they are unconcerned what beast they offer him, so long as it has a heart.

But the prophet Malachi thunders with divine indignation and jealousy against such worshippers: 'Ye have brought that which was torn, and the lame, and the sick: should I accept this of your hand? I am a great King, saith the Lord of hosts, and my name is dreadful' (*Mal.* 1:13–14). He upbraids us with sharp resentment; he tells us to offer it to our governor and asks if he would be pleased with it. Now our consciences sufficiently teach us to take care when we make an address to an earthly governor, to have our thoughts well ordered and words well chosen, and to offer it with a loyal heart. May not our supreme governor in heaven expect a due care in ordering our thoughts and choosing our words, so far at least as to answer all the intents of prayer, and so far as is consistent with the necessity of so frequent addresses to him and of our other Christian duties?

The reputation of religion in the world depends much on the honourable discharge of the duty of prayer. There is an inward beauty in divine worship that consists in the devout temper of the worshippers and the living exercise of holy devotion; but God only, who sees the heart, is witness to this. There is also an outward beauty that arises from a decent and acceptable performance of all the parts of it that come within the notice of our fellow creatures, that those that observe us may be forced to acknowledge the excellency of religion in our practice of it.

Where worship is performed by immediate inspiration, a natural order of things and a becoming behaviour is required especially in him who leads the worship. This is the design of the apostle in his advice to the Corinthians, 'Let all things be done decently and in order' (*1 Cor.* 14:40); that is, Let there be found among you a prudent conduct, a regular and rational management in all the parts of worship, so as to give a natural beauty to human actions and give a visible glory to the acts of religion. Where this advice is followed, if the unlearned and unbeliever come into the assembly, they will fall down and worship God, and report that God is truly in you (verse 25). But if you are guilty of disorder in speaking, and break the rules of natural light and reason in uttering your inspirations, the unlearned and unbelievers will say you are mad, though your words may be the dictates of the Holy Spirit.

Much more does this apply to our common and ordinary performance of worship. When an unskilful person speaks in prayer with a heaviness and barrenness of thought, with low and improper language, with a false and offensive tone of voice, or when he accompanies his words with awkward gestures, what slanders are thrown upon our practice! A whole party of Christians is ridiculed, and the scoffer says we are mad. But when a minister or master of a family, with a fluency of devout sentiments and language, offers his petitions and praises to God in the name of all that are present, and observes all the rules of natural decency in his voice and gesture, how much credit is done to our profession, even in the opinion of those who have no kindness for our way of worship! And how effectively does such a performance refute the claimed necessity of imposing forms! How gloriously does it triumph over the slanders of the adversary, and force a conviction upon the mind that there is something divine and heavenly among us!

I cannot represent this in a better manner than is done by an ingenious author of the last age who, being a courtier in the reigns of the two brothers, Charles II and James II, can never be suspected of being a dissenter, the late Marquis of Halifax. This noble writer in a little book under a borrowed character gives his own sentiments of things. He tells us that he is

> far from relishing the irrelevant wanderings of those who pour out long prayers upon the congregation, and all from their own stock; a barren soil, which produces weeds instead of flowers. By this means they expose religion itself, rather than promote men's devotions. On the other side, there may be too great restraint put upon men whom God and nature have distinguished from their fellow labourers by blessing them with a better talent and by giving them not only good sense, but a powerful utterance, too, which has enabled them

to gush out upon the attentive congregation with a mighty stream of devout and unaffected eloquence. When a man so qualified, endued with learning, too, and above all, adorned with a good life, breaks out into a warm and well delivered prayer before his sermon, it has the appearance of a divine rapture. He raises and leads the hearts of his assembly in another manner than the most composed or best-studied form of set words can ever do. And the 'pray we's' who serve up all their sermons with the same garnishing, would look like so many statues or men of straw in the pulpit compared with those that speak with such a powerful zeal that men are tempted at the moment to believe heaven itself has dictated their words to them.

5. A FIFTH PERSUASIVE ARGUMENT *to seek the gift of prayer shall be drawn from the easiness of attaining it with the common assistance of the Holy Spirit. I call it easy in comparison of the long toil and difficulty that men go through in order to acquire a common knowledge in arts, sciences or trades in this world; but it is not to be expected without some pains and diligence.*

Some young persons may be so unwise as to make two or three bold attempts to pray in company before they have well learned to pray in secret. And finding themselves much at a loss and bewildered in their thoughts, or confused for want of presence of mind, they have abandoned all hopes and contented themselves with saying it is impossible. And as they have tempted God by rashly venturing upon such an act of worship without any due care and preparation, so they have afterward thrown the blame of their own sloth upon God himself, saying it is a mere gift of heaven, but God has not bestowed it upon me. This is as if a youth who had just begun to read logic should attempt immediately to dispute in a public school, and finding himself baffled and confounded, should cast away his book, renounce his studies and say, I shall never learn it, it is impossible. When we seek any attainment, we must begin regularly and go on gradually toward perfection with patience and labour. Let but the rules recommended in the second chapter of this treatise for acquiring the gift of prayer be duly followed, and I do not doubt that a Christian of ordinary capacity may in time gain enough of this skill as to answer the demands of his duty and his station.

Rather than be utterly destitute of this gift of prayer, I would make such an experiment as this: Once a month I would draw up a new prayer for myself in writing, for morning and evening, and for the Lord's Day, according to all parts of this duty described in the first chapter of this book, or out of the Scriptures that Mr Henry has collected in his *Method for Prayer*, which book I would recommend to all Christians. I would use it constantly all that month, yet never confining myself all along to those very same words, but giving myself liberty to put in or leave out, or enlarge according to the present workings of my heart or the occurrences of providence. Thus by degrees I would write less and less, at last setting down little more than heads or hints of thought or expression, just as ministers learn by degrees to leave off their sermon notes in preaching. I would try whether a year or two of this practice would not equip me with an ability in some measure to pray without this help, always making it one of my petitions that God would pour more of his Spirit upon me and teach me the skill of praying. And by such short notes and general heads of prayer well drawn up for children according to their years and knowledge, they may be taught to pray by degrees and begin before they are six years old.

OBJECTION: A Christian that loves his ease may try to abuse this proposal and say, 'If I may use this prayer of my own framing for a month together, why may I not use it all my life and so give myself no further trouble about learning to pray?'

ANSWER: i. I would first desire such a man to read over again of the great difficulties, mentioned in the second chapter, that arise from a perpetual use of forms and of the danger of confinement to them.

ii. I would say in the second place that the matter of prayer is almost infinite. It extends to everything we can have to communicate with our Maker, and it is impossible in a few pages to mention specifically even one tenth of the subjects of our conversation with God. But in drawing up new prayers every month, in time we may run through a great part of those subjects and grow by degrees to be habitually equipped for conversing with him on all occasions whatever. This can never be done by dwelling always upon one form or two. Children learning at school to read take out new lessons daily, that they may be able at last to read everything; they would not attain this if they always dwelt on the same lesson.

iii. Moreover, there is a blessed variety of expressions in Scripture to represent our needs, sorrows and dangers, the glory, power and grace of God, his promises and covenant, our hopes and discouragements. Sometimes one expression, sometimes another, may best suit our present turn of thought and temper of our minds. It is good to have as large a supply of this kind as possible, that we might never be at a loss to express the inward sentiments of our soul and clothe our desires and wishes in words that are most exactly fitted to them.

iv. Though God is not the more affected with variety of words and arguments in prayer, for he acts upon other principles borrowed from himself, our own natures are more affected with such a variety. Our graces are drawn into more vigorous activity; by our importunity in pleading with God with many arguments we put ourselves more directly under the promise that is made to importunate petitioners; and we become fitter to receive the mercies we seek.

Yet I would make this concession: If we have the scheme and substance of several prayers ready composed and well suited to all the most usual cases and concerns of life and religion, and if one or other of these is daily used with seriousness – interposing new expressions wherever the soul is drawn out to further stirrings after God or where it finds occasion for new content from some present providence – this is much rather to be approved than a neglect of all prayer or a dwelling upon a single form or two. And it will be more edifying to those who join with us than a perpetual confusion of thought and endless dishonourable attempts in the more extemporary way.

But I say this by way of indulgence to persons of weaker gifts, or when the natural spirits are low or the mind much indisposed for duty. And in these cases this way of addressing God, which is called mixed prayer, will be so far from confining the pious soul to a dead form of worship that it will sometimes prove a sweet enlargement and release to the spirit from under its own darkness and confinement. It will supply it with spiritual content and awaken it to a longer and more lively conversation with God in its own language. If I may use a plain comparison, it will be like pouring a little water into a pump, and by doing so a much greater quantity will be raised from the spring when it lies low in the earth.

OBJECTION: A Christian on the other hand might forbid all use of such compositions as supposing them utterly unlawful and quenching the Spirit.

ANSWER: I would humbly reply that there is no danger of that while we do not rest in them as our intended end, but use them only as means to help us to pray, and never confine ourselves to them without liberty of alteration. It is the saying of a great divine, 'Though set forms made by others are as a crutch or help of our insufficiency, those which we compose ourselves are a fruit of our sufficiency. And that a man ought not to be so confined by any premeditated form as to neglect any special infusion, he should so prepare himself as if he expected no assistance, and he should so depend upon divine assistance as if he had made no preparation.'

Here, if I might have leave of my fathers in the ministry, I would say this to younger students: If in their private years of study they pursued such a course once a week as I have here described, I am persuaded their gifts would be richly developed; their ministerial labours would be more universally acceptable to the world; their talents would attract multitudes to their place of worship; the hearers would be raised in their spirits while the preacher prays with a regular and divine eloquence, and they would receive those sermons attended with such prayer with double influence and success.

6. THE LAST ATTEMPT *I shall make to convince Christians of the necessity of seeking this gift shall be merely by representing the ill consequences of its neglect. If you take no pains to learn to pray, you will unavoidably fall into one of these three evils:*

i. You will drag on heavily in the work of prayer all your days, even in your private rooms and with your family, and you will be liable to so many imperfections in the performance that it will rob your own soul of a great part of the benefit and the delight of this sweet duty and give neither pleasure nor profit to those who hear you. The ignorant part of your household will sleep under you, while the more knowing will be in pain for you. And perhaps you will sometimes think to make amends for the dullness of the devotion by increasing the length of it. But this is to add one error to another and lay more burdens upon those who are weary.

ii. Or, if you find that you cannot carry on the constancy of this duty with tolerable satisfaction, you will give yourself up to a morning and evening form and rest in them from year to year. Now though it may be possible for some persons to use a form without deadness and formality of spirit, still those who from mere sloth neglect to learn to pray are most likely to fall into formality and slothfulness in the use of forms, and the power of religion is lost.

iii. Or, if you have been brought up with a universal hatred of all forms of prayer and yet do not know how to pray without them, you will grow first inconstant in this duty, with every little hindrance diverting you; and at last perhaps you will leave it off entirely, and your house and your private room, too, in time will be without prayer.

Christians, which of these three evils will you choose? Can you be satisfied to drudge on to your life's end among improprieties and thus expose prayer to contempt? Or will your minds be satisfied to be confined forever to a form or two of slothful devotion? Or shall prayer be banished out of your houses and all appearance of religion lost among you?

Parents, which of these evils do you choose for your children? You charge them to pray daily, you tell them the sin and danger of dwelling all upon prayer books, and yet you scarcely ever give them any regular instructions on how to perform this duty. How can you expect them to maintain religion honourably in their families and avoid the things you forbid? But whatever ill consequences attend them hereafter, consider what share of the guilt will lie at the door of those who never took any pains to show them how to pray.

WHILE I AM PERSUADING Christians with so much earnestness to seek the gift of prayer, surely none will be so weak as to imagine that the grace and Spirit of prayer may be neglected. Without some degrees of common influence from the blessed Spirit, the gift is not to be attained. And without the activity of grace in this duty, the prayer will never reach heaven or prevail with God. He is not taken with the brightest forms of worship, if the heart is not there. The thoughts may be ever so divine, the expressions ever so sprightly and delivered with all the sweet and moving accents of speech, but it is all in his esteem only a beautiful carcass without a soul. It is a mere picture of prayer, a dead picture which cannot charm, a lifeless offering which the living God will never accept, nor will our great High Priest ever present it to the Father.

But these things do not fall directly under my present purpose. I would therefore recommend my readers to those treatises that enforce the necessity of spiritual worship and describe the glory of inward devotion above the best outward performances. Then shall they learn the perfection of beauty in this part of worship, when the gift and grace of prayer are happily joined in the secret pleasure and success of it, and appear before men in full loveliness and attractive power. Then shall religion look like itself, divine and heavenly, and shine in all the lustre it is capable of here upon earth.